LIEUTENANT NUN

LIEUTENANT NUN

MEMOIR OF A BASQUE TRANSVESTITE IN THE NEW WORLD

Catalina de Erauso

Translated from the Spanish by
Michele Stepto and Gabriel Stepto
Foreword by Marjorie Garber

Beacon Press   *Boston*

Beacon Press

25 Beacon Street

Boston, Massachusetts 02108-2892

Beacon Press books

are published under the auspices of

the Unitarian Universalist Association of Congregations.

19 18 17 16 15   19 18

Text and ornament design by Margaret M. Wagner

Composition by Wilsted & Taylor

Library of Congress Cataloging-in-Publication Data

Erauso, Catalina de, b. ca. 1592.

[Historia de la Monja Alférez. English]

Lieutenant nun : memoir of a Basque transvestite in the New World /

Catalina de Erauso ; translated from the Spanish by Michele Stepto

and Gabriel Stepto ; foreword by Marjorie Garber.

p.   cm.

ISBN 0-8070-7072-6 (cloth)

ISBN 0-8070-7073-4 (paper)

1. Erauso, Catalina de, b. ca. 1592.   2. Spain—Biography.   3. Latin America—
Biography.   I. Stepto, Michele.   II. Stepto, Gabriel.   III. Title.

CT1358.E7A3   1995

946'.052'092—dc20

[B]   95-8298

*for Robert and Rafael
and for Carlos, in memoriam*

FOREWORD
The Marvel of Peru

Another world was searched through oceans new
To find the *Marvel of Peru*;
And yet these rarities might be allowed
To man, that sovereign thing and proud,
Had he not dealt between the bark and tree,
Forbidden mixtures there to see.

—*ANDREW MARVELL,*
"The Mower Against Gardens" (1681)

H*ow can we* assess the erotic, social, and political effects of cross-dressing at a remove of almost four centuries, in the context of a culture very different from our own, and as described in a Spanish-language text? The short answer, of course, is that we can't. In the fascinating and fantastic adventures of the Lieutenant Nun doña Catalina de Erauso, who cross-dressed her way out of a Spanish convent and into the New World, what we read, what we find, is a version of ourselves.

When Catalina de Erauso fights duels, steals money, leads soldiers into battle, rescues a woman in distress, evades the marriage plans of hopeful widows and their daughters, and marches across league upon league of uncharted Peruvian terrain, it is tempting to see in her tale an allegory of early modern woman's emergent subjectivity. When, acting as a "second" for a friend whose honor has been insulted, she kills her brother unknowingly and inadvertently, it seems possible to see her as a version of Shakespeare's Viola in *Twelfth Night*, stepping into the shoes—and the clothing—of the brother she believes is dead. (It is a happy coincidence that her home-town in Spain is San Sebastian, the name of Viola's lost brother.) When Catalina flirts with two young women, "frol-icking" and "teasing," it might seem intriguing to read this as lesbianism *avant la lettre*, an instance of female homosexuality or, at the very least, love play between women. Yet all these readings are allegorical—that is to say, they are readings of her story as a story *about something else*, readings that offer her life—as indeed saints' and others' lives have been offered in the literary annals of her time and ours—as *exempla*, as indi-cations of deeper or higher truths.

Such modern readings are no more allegorical, it is perhaps needless to say, than the readings offered within the text it-self: the search for the king on Holy Thursday that culmi-nates in his discovery on Easter, the revelation that after all her adventuring (and horseback-riding) the Lieutenant Nun remains *virgo intacta*, the close-calls (or clothes-calls? or close-shaves?) in which she encounters first her father, then her mother, shortly after her cross-dressed flight from the confines of the convent, and neither parent recognizes her. She is already someone else. As a story about emergent sub-jectivity, male or female, early modern or postmodern, Cata-lina de Erauso's narrative is a literal description of self-fashioning, in which, quite literally, clothes make the man.

We may ourselves mistake subject for object, or discourse for subjectivity, when we regard Catalina's "self" as stable, and her costumes and roles as shifting. One thing that is very striking about this memoir is the materiality of clothing, and its value. Recall that this is a time period far removed from the mass production of garments and the availability of ready-to-wear. Clothing was wealth, and even identity. Actors in the theater wore noblemen's hand-me-downs, and were criticized for social climbing, a transvestism of rank or status as well as of gender. Catalina's payment from benefactors and employers is frequently a suit of clothes, and she describes these gifts with distinct pleasure and gratitude. They help to transform her, again quite literally, into another person, with a new status as well as a new gender. Clothes offer sensuous pleasure, wealth, status, and social roles.

Leaving the convent Catalina says she "shook off my veil" and spent three days and nights (the Christological interval is perhaps not inadvertent) re-making herself anew, cutting a pair of breeches from her blue woollen bodice, a doublet and hose from her green petticoat. Not long after this transformation, she describes herself finding work "as a page" and resembling "a well-dressed young bachelor."

Pages are often described in Renaissance literature as beautiful young boys who looked (almost) like girls, and could be regarded as sexual partners for men as well as women. Malvolio in Shakespeare's *Twelfth Night* correctly "reads" Viola's "femininity" when she is dressed as the boy Cesario, though he doesn't realize what he sees. A male page in *The Taming of the Shrew* is dressed in women's clothes and pretends to be the wife of the drunken tinker, Christopher Sly. The fantastical Spaniard Don Armado in *Love's Labour's Lost* rehearses his love-discourse with a page in the court of Navarre. In the Forest of Arden Rosalind chooses as her alias "no worse a name than Jove's own page" (*As You Like It* 1.3.124), and the name she adopts is "Ganymede," a slang term in the period for "boy lover" or "male prostitute." Since on the English public stage during the Renaissance female parts were played by boy actors, a complex eroticism attends these impersonations. Rosalind as Ganymede at the height of the plot's foolery is a boy (actor) playing a girl playing a boy playing a girl. "Madam, undress you, and come now to bed," says Christopher Sly to the page he thinks is his wife, only reluctantly agreeing, at the last minute, to substitute a stage-play for immediate love play "in despite of the flesh and the blood."

In the "real life" situations of Renaissance courtesans and prostitutes, who—for example, in Venice—often dressed as boys, the *frisson* of gender undecidability might be reversed, with provocative results for the flesh and the blood. "You talk like a fair lady and act like a pageboy," wrote the sixteenth-century author Pietro Aretino approvingly to a courtesan in the Italian town of Pistoia. Masculine clothing was stylish not only in Renaissance Italy but also in England and in France, where in the sixteenth century no less a personage than Marguerite de Navarre was described as both handsomely and bewilderingly attired: "You cannot tell whether she is male or female. She could just as well be a charming boy as the beautiful lady that she is."[1]

In a later time period equally titillated by gender crossover, Lady Caroline Lamb sat for her portrait in the costume of a page, and appeared in that guise at the door of her lover, the romantic poet Lord Byron. "He was a fair-faced delicate boy of thirteen or fourteen years old, whom one might have taken for the lady herself,"[2] a visitor reported of the cheeky young "page." In an instance of literature accompanying if not imi-

---

1. Pierre de Brantome, *La vie des dames galantes* (Paris).

2. R. C. Dallas, *Correspondence of Lord Byron with a Friend* (Paris: Galignani, 1825), pp. 41–42.

tating life, Byron's poem *Lara* centers on a male page who is revealed to be a girl, with a hand "So femininely white it might bespeak/Another sex."

The cultural and erotic fascination with pages, their borderline genders and sexualities (together with the literary and sexual fantasy of "turning the page"), continued on through the early twentieth century. In the 1920s lesbian poet Renée Vivien, dressed as a page, posed for a photograph with her lover Natalie Barney. Pageboy haircuts were the standard feminine style for conventional women in the 1950s (the same period that favored so-called "little boy" leg-styles on women's tailored bathing suits). Where the page was once a young man who could be taken for a young woman, he/she had become, by the early part of this century, a young woman who resembled an elegant if somewhat anachronistic young man.

But in the Catholic Spain of the seventeenth century the cross-dressed woman might have other valences and associations besides, or instead of, erotic ones. While England banned women from the stage, permitted transvestite actors, and feared that cross-dressing might provoke homosexual desire, Spain allowed women on the stage, rejected the use of transvestite boy players, and punished homosexuality with death. Female cross-dressing seems to have been viewed with particular concern, since it was banned a number of times— for example, in 1600, 1608, 1615, and 1641. (The ban, obviously, proved ineffective, since it needed so frequently to be renewed.)[3] Pedro Calderón de la Barca's *La vida es sueño* (*Life*

---

3. Ursula K. Heise, "Transvestism and the Stage Controversy in Spain and England, 1580–1680," *Theatre Journal* 44.3 (October 1992), p. 357. Stephen Orgel, "Nobody's Perfect: Or Why Did the English Stage Take Boys for Women?" in *Displacing Homophobia*, ed. Ronald R. Butters, John M. Clum, and Michael Moon, *South Atlantic Quarterly* 88.1 (Winter 1989), p. 28.

Is a Dream), a play dated around 1636, features a cross-dressed woman determined to avenge her own honor, in the tradition of *pundonor*. "As a man I come to serve you bravely / Both with my person and my steel," Rosaura tells the prince to whom she has revealed her true identity. "If you today should woo me as a woman / Then I should have to kill you as a man would / In honourable service of my honour."[4] The medieval Catholic example of Joan of Arc, the cross-dressed soldier and saint tried for transvestism by the Inquisition, is never invoked in the memoir, nor is the more distant but equally pertinent example of Saint Uncumber or Wilgefortis, known as Librada in Spain, the "redeemer of women from men," of whom it is said that, to protect her virgin status, she prayed for Christ's help and was immediately adorned with a moustache and beard; her intended husband, the pagan king of Sicily, declined to marry her but her father had her crucified. Where Joan and Librada both differ signally from Catalina de Erauso, of course, is that neither ever tried to pass as a man.

In the course of her long career as an itinerant soldier of fortune, Catalina is once stripped and placed on the rack, and on several other occasions her wounds are tended by benevolent strangers. Why does she never express a fear of detection? Wouldn't the stripping reveal aspects of her female anatomy, her woman's body? For a modern reader, much of the suspense initially inheres in the constant risk that her "secret" will be discovered. But these are questions she does not explore and worries she does not manifest. (The episode on the rack seems to have produced no disquieting revelation,

4. Pedro Calderón de la Barca, *Life is a Dream*, trans. Roy Campbell, in *Six Spanish Plays*, ed. Eric Bentley (New York: Doubleday Anchor, 1959), act 3, ll. 490–94.

since on receiving a note urging clemency the justice instructs the torturers to "take the lad down.") But Catalina de Erauso is much more concerned about self-exposure with people she *knows*: her mother, her father, her brother. It is these persons alone who can return her to an identity she has by now set aside, or moved beyond.

And what about her own erotic life? She says virtually nothing about it. From a modern perspective gender disguise looks to many readers like a transparent narrative about sexuality and eroticism. But we have in the memoir no articulation of longing, no sense of entrapment in gender disguise, no relief at avoiding male attentions, no sustained temptation to engage in courtship or to take a lover or a mate. Catalina's story does not seem to be about "sex," at least as she tells it. No man ever suspects Catalina's female identity, or makes a pass at her either as a man or as a woman. The threat of marriage with a half-breed widow's daughter or an eager churchman's niece precipitates a little crisis, but it is only a crisis in *narrative*. "I saddled up and vanished." The flirtatious and overly familiar whores at the memoir's end are dismissed out of hand as "harlots" whose honor only a fool would defend. As she tells it, hers is the story of a loner who enjoys camaraderie with men, an adventurer who spends most of her peripatetic career in the New World, yet whose proudest claim to identity is not as a man or a woman but rather as a "Spaniard."

In England the Puritan pamphleteer William Prynne was one of many who inveighed against cross-dressing on the stage as a transgression sure to produce immoral desire. During his trial for sedition in the 1630s, Prynne's disparaging view of contemporary hairdressing styles was read aloud to the court.

Identifiable gender markings, he had complained, were per-
versely undone by contemporary fashion. Men curled their
long hair, while "our Englishe gentle-women, as yf they all
intended to turn men outright, and weare the breeches, or to
be Popish nunnes, are now growne soe farr past shame, past
modesty, grace, and nature, as to clipp their hayre like men,
with lockes and foretoppes." Cutting their hair, English-
women became—or "intended to turn"—either "men" or
"nuns." In either case, the strongly anti-Catholic Prynne
maintained, they were behaving against nature.

Yet surprisingly, in the case of the Lieutenant Nun, who
becomes *both* a "man" *and* a "nun" in the course of her adventures, no strong sense of moral outrage is expressed by those
who learn her secret, no sense that she is "unnatural" or behaving "against nature." In Seville, she became a celebrity.
Rather than cross-dressing, the sins for which she needs ab-
solution are more likely to be fighting, brawling, gambling,
and murder.

In my book *Vested Interests: Cross-Dressing and Cultural
Anxiety* (HarperCollins, 1993), I describe the literary and
cultural phenomenon I call a "category crisis" and a related
manifestation I call the "transvestite effect." A category crisis
is a failure of definitional distinction, a borderline that becomes permeable, permitting border crossings from one apparently distinct category to another. What seems like a bi-
nary opposition, a clear choice between opposites that define
cultural boundaries, is revealed to be not only a construct but
also—more disturbingly—a construct that no longer works to
contain and delimit meaning. Some examples pertinent to
Catalina's story might include male/female, black/white, gay/
straight, Christian/Indian, Christian/cannibal, Old World/

New World, master/servant, master/slave. The appearance of a transvestite figure in a text, I suggest—whether that "text" be an artifact of fiction, history, narrative, or visual culture—was almost invariably a sign of a category crisis *elsewhere*: not, or not only, in the realms of gender and sexuality, but also, and equally importantly, in registers like politics, economics, history, and literary genre. Since from the point of view of a modern, twentieth-century readership gender and sexuality are often regarded as a kind of "ground" of identity and identity-formation, these transvestite figures mark the narratives in which they appear as narratives of a world under conceptual stress. And the more extraneous the fact of cross-dressing appears to be to the story the text seems to be telling, the more critical the "crisis" of category, the more blurred the boundary that is being, apparently, policed.

After Catalina is nursed to health by a lady she describes as a "half-breed" in Tucumán," the daughter of a Spaniard and an Indian woman, a widow and a good woman," the stage is set for a category crisis. Indeed, she is remanded into the good woman's care by rescuers whose initial identity she doubts— "were they cannibals or Christians?" The woman's desire to have this apparently eligible young bachelor marry her daughter founders, not only on the bachelor's "real" gender identity but also on questions of race and beauty. It is perfectly possible that among the non-narrated escapades of the memoir (Catalina will say much later that "a few other things happened to me . . . but since they don't add up to much I omit them from these pages") is, or rather might have been, some evidence of (homo)sexual desire. But as it stands the resistance to marriage is more strongly marked by aversions of class, race, and nobility than by gender or sexuality. The transvestite effect is powerful in part because it seems both "the point" of the story and somehow something "beside the point."

Catalina de Erauso's Basque identity is another such border crossing. She and her family are proud that they come from the Basque country, a region on the borderline between Spain and France with its own distinct language and culture. More than once in the New World her escape from a tight spot is facilitated by a fellow Basquero. The disruptive gender identities (marked in the text by "male" and "female" pronouns) and geographical wandering between Spain and Peru are undertaken by a figure already exceptional and transgressive, whose nationality is as complex as her personal history.

Tensions between Old and New World, between Indians and "Spaniards," between purebreds and "half-breeds," and between the merchant class and the nobility put under increasing pressure by the *encomienda* system of settlement and fealty could be said to have "produced" a triumphant story of transvestite transgression—or, at least, to have produced a sympathetic audience for such a tale. "News of this event [her confession] had spread far and wide, and it was a source of amazement to the people who had known me before, and to those who had only heard of my exploits in the Indies, and to those who were hearing of them for the first time." Catalina's celebrity was not only a sign of personal distinction; it was, as she tells it, an effect of paradox, risk, and excess. If, as Michele Stepto has said in the introduction to Catalina's memoirs, "in Peru, as everywhere else in the Americas, abundance tended to dissolve ancient links between power and hereditary status," this was the very kind of category crisis for which a transvestite heroine (and, moreover, one both impeccably virginal and commendably patriotic) was emblematically ideal, a "marvel of Peru."

The poem by Andrew Marvell quoted at the beginning of this foreword is spoken by a mower who deplores the growing seventeenth-century taste in gardening, the desire to alter and "improve" on nature by grafting ("forbidden mixtures") and by importing flowers from the New World. (The "Marvel of Peru" [*mirabilis jalapa*], also known as "Beauty-in-the-Night" and "four-o'clock," a staple of modern gardens, was at the time an exotic flower.) This was a major topos in both seventeenth-century gardening and seventeenth-century poetry (Shakespeare's Perdita has a quarrel with the disguised King Polixenes along the same lines in *The Winter's Tale*), and it was often taken, as the "garden" figure suggests, as a description of both an ideal and a desecrated Eden, with serious political implications.

In what are perhaps the best-known lines of the poem, the mower laments the ambition of "luxurious man":

> No plant now knew the stock from which it came;
> > He grafts upon the wild the tame,
> That the uncertain and adulterate fruit
> > Might put the palate in dispute.
> His green seraglio has its eunuchs, too,
> > Lest any tyrant him outdo;
> And in the cherry he does Nature vex,
> > To procreate without a sex.

The mower's conservative resistance to "forbidden mixtures" and "uncertain and adulterate fruit" (precisely the titillating transgressions that excited modern garden enthusiasts of the period) may be pertinently juxtaposed to the vogue for cross-dressing and cross-dressing narratives, on the stage, in the streets, and in the annals of popular culture, were "forbidden mixtures" and the intergrafting of "wild" and "tame" the end of civilization as the old garden knew and embodied it, or the beginning of a brilliant and tumultuous new future?

The anxieties of "adultery," the power of the "eunuch," and the dark fantasy of procreation without a sex appear in numerous undercover forms in *Lieutenant Nun*, all translated into figures for economic as well as erotic violation. The chief insult is "cuckold"; the scenario for a fight is the gaming table. Questions of property rather than propriety are paramount. Catalina, miraculously herself still a virgin, eluding the claims of her "natural" parents and family, confounds the "forbidden mixtures" of gender, sexuality, class, and nation to emerge as a sign of Spain's—and Catholicism's—primacy in a changing and mysterious world. No wonder the king was willing to grant her a pension, and the Pope a dispensation.

A study of female transvestism in early modern Europe by Dutch scholars Rudolf Dekker and Lotte van der Pol records the stage popularity of plays about "the Spaniard Catalina de Erauso and the Englishwoman Mary Frith." As they note, "female soldiers had a propaganda value: the monarch could show to the world that even women rallied under his banners," and the example they cite is that of Catalina de Erauso, who lived "a life as a conquistador in South America, where she not only had not behaved like a lady, but in fact not like a gentleman either."[5] Not like a lady and not like a gentleman:

5. Rudolf M. Dekker and Lotte C. van der Pol, *The Tradition of Female Transvestism in Early Modern Europe* (New York: St. Martin's Press, 1989), pp. 95–96.

as this formulation suggests, gendered behavior in what likes to think of itself as polite society is not "natural," but rather a series of adaptive roles. Catalina, quite literally neither the one thing nor the other, carved out for herself the freedom to transgress, and—like the most successful gender-benders of today's popular culture and the arts—was rewarded for her temerity, however briefly, with fame and money.

New World narratives that engage the question of cross-dressing tend to locate it within the practice of the Indians rather than the Spanish. "Cross-dressed bodies," writes Jonathan Goldberg (analyzing an early account of Balboa's visit to an Indian king whose brother and other young male courtiers were said to be dressed in "womens apparell"), "are the locus of identity and difference, a site for crossings between Spanish and Indians, and for divisions between and among them."[6] In the case of Catalina de Erauso, however, the cross-dresser is female, not male, virile, not effeminate, Spanish, not Indian, and virginal, not dissolute.

Accounts of women who dressed as men have proven to be engaging reading for a late twentieth-century public interested in, even obsessed with, the fluidity (and limits) of its own gender and erotic roles. Julia Wheelright's 1989 *Amazons and Military Maids*, for example, contained accounts of numerous English, Irish, American, and Russian women who "dressed as men in pursuit of life, liberty and happiness" and served as soldiers, sailors, and pirates from the eighteenth century to the twentieth, among them Hannah Snell, who became James Gray, a British soldier and sailor in the eighteenth

---

6. Jonathan Goldberg, *Sodometries: Renaissance Texts, Modern Sexualities* (Stanford: Stanford University Press, 1992), p. 184.

century; Christian Davies, an Irish publican turned soldier; Maria Bochkareva, the leader of the Russian Women's Battalion of Death; Deborah Sampson, who fought during the American Revolution disguised as Robert Shurtleff; Angélique Brulon, a soldier in Napoleon's infantry; and Valerie Arkell-Smith, otherwise known as Colonel Barker. Mary Fleming Zurin's translation of the journals of a Russian officer in the Napoleonic wars, published in 1988 under the title *The Cavalry Maiden*, chronicled the story of Nadezhda Durova, a cross-dressed hussar officer who served in the cavalry for ten years as "Aleksandr Andrevich Aleksandrov." In her hussar role Durova confesses herself "shy" before women and the butt of jokes from the wives and daughters of fellow officers, who "never miss a chance to make me blush by calling me *hussar miss* as a joke"—not comprehending that their "joke" is a kind of truth. "A woman has only to look fixedly at me to start me blushing in confusion," she writes. "I feel as if she sees right through me and guesses my secret from my appearance alone."[7] Like Catalina at the end of her story, Nadezhda was known in her female identity to the monarch, in this case Czar Alexander I of Russia, who granted her the commission.

Michele Stepto and Gabriel Stepto have enterprisingly opted to use the idiom of the American West in rendering Catalina's story, reminding the reader that "Peru was on the western frontier of Spain's New World empire." They cite Huck Finn as a rhetorical model. Another obvious figure from the annals of "the West" might be the legendary cross-dressed American frontierswoman Calamity Jane, also known as

7. Nadezhda Durova, *The Cavalry Maiden*, trans. Mary Fleming Zurin (Bloomington: Indiana University Press, 1988), p. 78.

Martha Jane Burke, whose raucous history in Deadwood, South Dakota, was entwined with that of Wild Bill Hickok. An even closer analogue, however—since Calamity Jane married and had a subsequent public career as a woman in Wild West shows—might be the kind of cross-dressed Western pioneer who lived as a man, like the eponymous hero/heroine of the 1993 film *The Ballad of Little Jo*.

Jo (played by Suzy Amis) escapes from her repressive Eastern family and a romance gone awry, donning men's clothes as a way of avoiding men's advances as she works her way toward a rough-and-tumble mining town in the West. Achieving acceptance as a man in a man's world, Jo also finds love and sexuality in a secret relationship with a Chinese-American man she takes on as a hired hand; his marginal status (Asian, itinerant, subservient) balances her own, and provides the set of category crises out of which the film crafts its possibility for boundary-breaking romance. As so often in such stories her "real" gender identity is publicly disclosed only after her death, when the undertaker comes to lay out the body.

The Ballad of Little Jo, directed by a woman, Maggie Greenwald, is ultimately a tale of female heterosexual independence, with far more in the way of "love story" than *Lieutenant Nun*. But another signature story of the American West with a similar dénouement (the autopsy surgeon discovers the female body) tells a slightly different tale. The story is that of Jack Bee Garland, writer, newspaperman, and social worker, who was identified on his death in 1936 as "the long-vanished" Elvira Virginia Mugarrieta, daughter of San Francisco's first Mexican consul, granddaughter of a Louisiana Supreme Court Justice. "She wanted to go to the Philippines in 1899 to see the Spanish-American war front there," reported Elvira's sister. "She couldn't go as a woman, so . . .

she put on men's clothes, went over on an army transport with a Colorado regiment, and served as a field hospital worker."[8] After her death—described with unconscious wit by the *Oakland Tribune* as "her passing"—reporters discovered that Jack Bee Garland had had another life in the 1890s as a woman called Babe Bean, an eccentric denizen of Stockton's high society, who dressed in male clothing but made no secret of her gender, and was "accompanied by a male companion." Interrogated by the Stockton police, Babe said of her male clothing, "It is my only protection; I do it because I am alone."[9]

Jack Bee's biographer, transgender activist Louis Sullivan, describes him as "a female-to-male transsexual, even though such luxuries as modern-day male hormone therapy and sex reassignment surgeries were not available options during his lifetime."[10] One can almost imagine such a sentence being written about Catalina de Erauso, who ended her life as the Mexican mule-driver Antonio de Erauso. But the degree of anachronistic dislocation involved in such a diagnosis— across centuries, cultures, and gaps in knowledge—should serve as a warning against any temptation to assimilate individual life-stories toward coherent master narratives. We read from where we are, and from our own cultural and historical position. All our reading is in a sense misreading or overreading. What I want to emphasize here is that such overdetermination is part of the pleasure of reading as well as part of its danger. *All* reading is *partial* in two senses—not *im*partial and not whole.

8. Louis Sullivan, *From Female to Male: The Life of Jack Bee Garland* (Boston: Alyson Publications, 1990), p. 9.
9. Ibid., p. 17.
10. Ibid., p. 3.

In this engrossing and elegantly translated memoir the reader is afforded a glimpse into a world almost unimaginably alien and estranging. Yet it is at the same time a world whose insistent if limited analogies to modern (and postmodern) experience are seductively present. The effect of the first-person memoir, even mediated through the translators' text, is disarmingly engaging and direct. If self-consciously "modern" categories like race, class, gender, sexuality, nation, and religion are all at work in this narrative—and they are—their mutual interplay is far from predictable. What emerges is a clear and complex voice telling a story that can be read at once as autobiography and pilgrimage, picaresque and memoir.

Ultimately the question of "gender" as a category of analysis within seventeenth-century Spanish and New World culture remains a space of negotiation rather than a set of knowable answers. We might compare it to the constant repetition in the memoir of the word "league." In almost every chapter Catalina records her travels: "I left Tucumán . . . and made my way to Potosí some five hundred and fifty leagues away"; "I had no choice but to leave La Plata, and I headed for Charcas some sixteen leagues off"; "they flung me and my two companions out on the Paita coast, a good hundred leagues from Lima." How long is a league? Land leagues of about 2.63 miles were used by the Spanish in early surveys of parts of the American Southwest, but the term "league" is extremely various and contingent in its definitions, ranging from 2.4 to 4.6 statute miles (3.9 to 7.4 kilometers) by some reckonings. In English-speaking countries the league is often equivalent to three statute miles; in ancient Rome it was 1,500 paces; in the eighteenth century a league was defined as the distance a cannon shot could be fired at enemy ships offshore. In a modern lexicon in which "league" has taken on some aspects of the fantastic or the marvelous ("seven-league boots"), the league, a common Spanish measure, seems in Catalina's account of her progress both excessively precise and excessively general. Catalina's cross-dressing occupies, I want to suggest, the same double terrain of fact and fable. Its "truth" is both literal and allegorical. In *Lieutenant Nun*, Catalina de Erauso emerges as a figure at once male and female, enigmatic and familiar, resolute and endangered, abject and celebrated, elusive and recognizable—a figure, we might say, in a league of her own.

MARJORIE GARBER

INTRODUCTION

It *is more than ten years now* since an Argentine friend presented me with a photocopy of the 1918 edition of Catalina de Erauso's *La Historia de la Monja Alférez*, but I remember her description of the book as if it were yesterday. "It's about a nun who fled the convent," she said, "and lived the life of a bandit for many years, posing as a man, until one day she was apprehended at a crossroads and given a choice—she could return to the convent and set down her confession in writing, or she could be tried and hanged for her crimes. She chose to confess, and this is the confession she wrote."

As I read *La Historia*, I looked in vain for the eloquent details of my friend's synopsis—the crossroads, the choice that was no choice at all, the confession, the resubmersion beneath the veil—delighted, but also perplexed, to discover in the book in hand the story of a woman who had lived freely, given the time and place, and more or less escaped the consequences. Later, as I learned more about the history of this woman, I understood that my friend's version belonged to the body of lore and legend that had developed around the figure of Catalina de Erauso, and that had taken on a vivid life of its own in the 150 years during which her memoir remained unpublished.

For centuries, the Spanish-speaking world has been fascinated by the story of the Basque girl with the quick temper who ran away from her convent dressed as a man and became La Monja Alférez, the Lieutenant Nun. To summarize the highpoints of her life—as she herself set them down in her memoir—is to rehearse the tale of a picaro let loose on the New World: She traveled to the Americas in 1603, became a soldier, fought in the conquest of Chile. She enjoyed the attentions of other women, killed her brother in a duel, gambled and brawled her way through the mining towns of the Andean highlands. She killed and maimed, spent time in jail, and more time in the sanctuary of the Church. She claimed the privilege of nobility to escape torture, and proclaimed herself a heretic to escape hanging. When finally cornered, after twenty years of masking, she revealed her secret—she was not only a woman, but an intact virgin, a piece of news that, far from condemning her, brought her a brief celebrity in the Baroque world. In 1624, she returned to Europe, where she earned from the Spanish king a military pension, and from the pope permission to continue her life in men's clothing. Then, in 1630, she returned to the new world, and slipped from the pages of history.

Catalina de Erauso began life in the town of San Sebastian, on the northern coast of Spain, a middle child and the third daughter of a large and prosperous Basque family. She gives 1585 as the year of her birth, though records in San Sebastian indicate she was baptized in 1592. In either case, she was born into a Spain that was enjoying its first hundred years of American conquest, and extending that conquest further and further south along the western coast of South America, a Spain that had dedicated itself, its sons, its military and commercial activity to the harvest of riches in lands thousands of miles away. Whatever Catalina may have come to know in the years before she herself left for the Americas, she must have been keenly aware of there being another world, a "new"

world. Of those far shores, she must have heard countless
stories.

Her father, Captain Miguel de Erauso, had probably
served in the American colonies. Her older brother Miguel
had been there since Catalina was two—"I had had news of
him," she remembers. Three more brothers, Domingo, Francisco, and Martín, would follow him there, and all four would
end their lives in South America. But while the Erauso sons
went forth into the expanding world, a different future was
unfolding for the Erauso daughters. Like other prosperous
Basque families, the Erausos gave their sons to the conquest
and their daughters to the convent, thus promoting the family prestige and protecting its honor. One by one, the girls
entered the convent of San Sebastián the Elder, there to
be reared and educated—for marriage if a likely match presented itself, for a nun's life if it did not.

Conventional marriage or the conventual life—these
were the possibilities open to the Erauso daughters, among
whom Mariana eventually married, while Mari Juana, Isa-
bel, and Jacinta lived out their lives in the town convent.
Catalina alone escaped, and in a way that tells us much
about the freedom available to Spanish men of her class, and
much about her own versatility. She refashioned her under-
garments into a suit of men's clothes, cut her hair short, and
walked out of San Sebastián. In the neighboring town of Vitoria, she presented herself as a young servant, and thereafter as a page to the king's secretary, as a mysterious young
bachelor in her hometown, and finally as ship's boy to her un-
witting uncle, in whose galleon she crossed the Atlantic. In
Nombre de Dios, as her uncle readied his galleon for the return voyage to Spain, stowing the gold that was the fruit of

Spanish conquest, Catalina stole what she needed from him and jumped ship, setting out to make her way alone in the New World.

Everything in Catalina's memoir bespeaks a quick and enterprising nature, a spirited, often ungovernable temper, a love of action and travel. Given such qualities, it is no wonder that she chose to don men's clothing and follow her father and brothers to the Americas. But the Peruvian world she was to make her way in would, in many ways, have been utterly familiar to Catalina. Though unimaginably distant, it was nevertheless recognizably Spanish.

In 1603, when Catalina came to Peru, the Hispanicization of the region was an accomplished fact. The defeat of the Incan empire by Francisco Pizarro and his followers was not even three-quarters of a century old, yet the mechanisms whereby imperial Spain would subdue much of the region's Indian population and exploit its extraordinary natural riches were firmly in place. The major cities of present-day Peru, Ecuador, and Bolivia—then all part of Greater Peru—had already been founded, many of them rising, like Quito and Cuzco, in places from which the Inca had held sway. The Catholic missionary orders had long been on the scene, proselytizing the crown's new Indian subjects and founding churches, schools, hospitals, monasteries, and convents, including the *grandes conventos* of Lima, like La Santísima Trinidad, where Catalina spent two and a half years before returning to Spain. A thriving merchant and artisan class, by now several generations old, was keeping Spanish Peruvians supplied with military equipment and the finest domestic luxuries their wealth could buy.

Above all, Spain's distinctive land-grant system had already carved up much of the inhabited landscape into nearly five hundred administrative units, or *encomiendas*. Under the *encomienda* system, the grantee received not land itself but the tribute of Indians residing within certain boundaries. In return for the promise to protect and Christianize his Indian *encomendados*, and to marry and take up residence in one of the Spanish Peruvian cities, the *encomendero* grew rich, often fabulously rich, from the tribute of his Indian workers. As the mineral wealth of the Andes began to be reckoned, and especially following the discovery of the great silver mountain of otosí in 1545, a scant seven years after the Conquest, Indian ibute began to be exacted in the form of labor, with gangs of *itayos* or conscripted Indian workers moved from one mining site to another. The wealth which Indian labor produced, in both mine and field, allowed the *encomendero* and his wife to enrich their families back home while, in the urban centers of Greater Peru, they maintained large households of relatives, retainers, servants, and African slaves, households where Spanish custom, language, and religious practice were the rule. Thus, the system whereby Andean riches were funneled back to Spain simultaneously insured the firm planting of Spanish culture in the far western reaches of South America, on shores no European had guessed at a mere eighty years before. By the time Catalina arrived there, the very name Peru had come to mean fabulous wealth. But the riches that drew people from all over the Spanish empire, and beyond, also made for the attenuation of age-old Spanish custom in the new kingdom. Practices evolved to keep scarce wealth in the hands of a stable few will not remain unchanged in a place where scarcity—of land, of the labor to work it, of precious metals—is hardly the order of the day. In Peru, as everywhere else in the Americas, abundance tended to dissolve ancient links between power and hereditary status.

Moreover, many of Peru's early conquerors were men of plebeian roots, transformed by the reward of rich *encomiendas* into the governing elite of the new kingdom. By the same token, Spanish Peruvian women, vastly outnumbered by men in the early colonial period, often elevated their status considerably through marriage to newly made *encomenderos*, who were duty-bound to take Spanish wives. By old-world standards, this could make for a certain social topsy-turviness, the kind of disorder we catch a glimpse of in chapter 10, in the violent dispute between doña Francisca Marmolejo, highborn and well-connected, and doña Catalina de Chaves, whose plebeian name connects her to Francisco de Chaves, Pizarro's friend and one of the early conquerors. While the gift of *encomiendas* was soon expended, so that by the midsixteenth century few new ones were being granted, in the chaotic world of Peru every Spaniard who came afterward, even the humblest baker or foot soldier, could expect to improve his or her condition in ways impossible to those who stayed at home.

Like all rich frontiers, like the Old West, Peru drew adventurers of every stripe. The region was crammed with gamblers and other itinerant types who, because they had little or nothing at stake, were a constant threat to colonial order. From time to time the powers-that-were rounded some of them up, paid them 200 *pesos* each, and sent them off on expeditions—or *entradas*—meant to subdue distant Indian villages and take new land for Spain. More often than not, the *entradas* ended in disaster, most notoriously in the case of the 1560 Amazonian expedition of Pedro de Orsua and the Basquero Lope de Aguirre. But the practice was still in use in

1605, when Catalina, suddenly friendless and unemployed, accepted 280 pesos to fight in Chile. Although she distinguished herself in the Araucanian Wars of Chile, rising to the rank of second lieutenant, Catalina's service did not procure any immediate change in her status. Her hand-to-mouth existence as a soldier continued and, following the accidental killing of her brother, she took up full rank in the itinerant underclass.

Catalina's detailed portrait of this class of Spanish Peruvians challenges the heroic version of the Conquest, but it jibes well enough with first-hand accounts of life on the Spanish colonial frontier. In his "Anonymous Description of Peru," Pedro de León Portocarrero, a Portuguese Jew who resided in Lima between 1600 and 1615, describes a world of "riots, disturbances, and untoward events" that is clearly the Peru Catalina moved in. His comparison of the Spanish Peruvian cardsharp and soldier offers a portrait of Peruvian life strikingly similar to Catalina's own. Portocarrero begins with the cardsharps:

> poor but haughty fellows; they can't bite but they can bark loudly. With heads low they go about sniffing for prey; they have no desire to subordinate themselves, nor is there any reasoning with them. Individuals of that sort are called "soldiers," not because they really are soldiers, but because they go hither and yon with a pack of cards in their hands and lose no opportunity to gamble with anyone they come across. If, by chance, they run into a novice or tenderfoot who is not very bright or whose suspicious nature does not extend to the possibility of a stacked pack of cards, they cheat him out of his money and possessions; sometimes they even win his horse or mule from under him. They are

consummate tricksters whose only concern is to master the art of deception. . . .

A different and less numerous breed take to soldiering, since every year recruits are sent from Lima to Chile. This type is not so clever, nor so free and easy in the art of flattery, and they lack the means to wander from one region to another like tramps. Usually they are slightly more disposed to accept employment, especially in the exercise of arms, by which they can live off the king's bounty. This element marches off with banners flying to fight against the Araucanian Indians after receiving 200 *pesos* in Lima with which to buy clothes. In this way the country is rid of them and troops are available to make war on the indomitable Araucanians. Few ever return to Peru.[1]

Portocarrero's description of the fate that awaited those who joined the army of conquest suggests that Catalina knew what she was doing when she left off soldiering to become a gambler.

After twenty years of knocking about Peru, increasingly the object of the law's attentions, Catalina revealed her secret to the young bishop of Guamanga with whom she had taken sanctuary, the "saintly" friar don Agustín de Carvajal, before whom she remembers "feeling as if I might already be in the presence of God." Undoubtedly, she also felt herself in a tight spot, but whatever her intentions the effect was immediate. She became an overnight wonder, and a week later, when

1. "Anonymous Description of Peru," in *Colonial Travelers in Latin America*, ed. William C. Bryant (Newark, Delaware: Juan de la Cuesta, 1972), pp. 98–99.

the bishop escorted her to the convent of Santa Clara, they couldn't enter the church, so great were the crowds that had gathered to see La Monja Alférez.

Catalina spent three years in Peruvian convents while the status of her religious vows was investigated. "Once again I donned the veil," is how she puts it, and while this sounds ominous, the interlude cannot have been altogether unpleasurable, considering her decided preference for the company of other women. When word finally came from Spain that she had never taken her final vows and was therefore free to go, she took an emotional leave of her companions at La Santísima Trinidad and stopped in Guamanga on her way back to Spain to spend a week with the nuns of Santa Clara.

Back in Europe, Catalina was characteristically and perpetually on the move, now celebrated, now obscure, and as disaster-prone as ever. In 1625, she presented a petition to the king, asking that he reward her "for the worthiness of her deeds and for the singularity and prodigiousness of her life, mindful that she is the daughter of noble and illustrious parents who are principal citizens in the town of San Sebastián; and for the rectitude and rare purity in which she has lived and lives, to which many have borne testimony; for which she would be honored to receive a yearly stipend of seventy pesos apportioned in 22 quilates per month in the city of Cartagena de las Indias, and funds to travel there . . ."[2] Already she was thinking of returning to the New World. During this same year, in Rome, she was introduced to the writer Pedro del Valle, who described her in a letter to a friend: "Tall and powerfully built, and with a masculine air, she has no more

---

2. "Petition of Catalina de Erauso to the Spanish Crown, 1625," trans. Stephanie Merrim, *Review: Latin American Literature and Arts*, no. 43 (1990), p. 37.

breasts than a girl. She told me that she had used some sort of remedy to make them disappear. I believe it was a poultice given her by an Italian—it hurt a great deal, but the effect was very much to her liking. Her face is not ugly, but very worn with years. Her appearance is basically that of a eunuch, rather than a woman. She dresses as a man, in the Spanish style. She carries her sword as bravely as she does her life."[3]

Sometime between 1626 and 1630—that is, between the visit to Naples, which concludes her memoir, and her return to the Americas—she wrote down in manuscript or dictated to an amanuensis an account of her life. As one might expect from someone of her time and place, whose life overlapped with Cervantes' by thirty years, her account is firmly shaped by the Spanish picaresque tradition, which flourished in the century and a half following the Colombian discovery. And like the better known classics of this tradition—the anonymously authored *Lazarillo de Tormes*, Mateo Alemán's *Guzmán de Alfarache*, Cervantes' *Rinconete y Cortadillo* and *Don Quijote*, Quevedo's *Vida del Buscón*, as well as Defoe's *Moll Flanders*—Catalina's memoir forcefully reminds us that the picaresque is a creature of discovery and conquest, a new mode of storytelling brought to birth in a suddenly vast and changing world. In her autobiography, as in so many other accounts of the time, fictional and nonfictional, the hand-to-mouth life of the commoner replaces the chivalric doings of nobility, while the symbolic terrain and conventional moral action of medieval romance give way to the startling factuality of real places and people.

3. Cited by José María de Heredia in his introduction to the 1918 edition of *La Historia de la Monja Alférez*, ed. Joaquín María de Ferrer (Madrid: Tipografía Renovación, 1918), p. vii.

Catalina's story is long on action and travel, on facts, names, and enumeration, because those are what she craved as a child of her age, what she left the convent of San Sebastian to discover. It is short on observation and self-examination because those are activities of leisure and quiet, conditions she willingly abandoned along with her veil. This emphasis on action, even on the verb as such, challenges the contemporary reader as well as the translator who wishes to make her memoir accessible in the here and now. Three sequences may serve as guides, however, to understanding Catalina's life as she told it.

In the first chapter, as she recounts wandering about the Spanish peninsula in the guise of a young man, Catalina speaks of herself as one without volition or strategy, "carried off like a feather in the wind." When her father arrives in Valladolid in search of her, she quietly slips off to Bilbao—"When I heard the anguish in my father's voice," she remembers, "I backed off slowly . . ." But when, "with no more reason than that it suited me," she leaves a comfortable situation in Estella to return to her hometown of San Sebastian, she discovers there that not even her own mother now recognizes her. In her typical low key, Catalina seems to downplay the moment—"I went to hear mass at my old convent, the same mass my mother attended, and I saw that when she looked at me she did not recognize me"—but this is a dramatic turning point in her young life, after which her travels take direction. Up to this point, she has insisted on her own lack of volition, but now, by a familiar psychological ruse, she discovers in her mother's unknowing glance her warrant for freedom—a warrant she may have been seeking when she returned to San Sebastian—and before long she is on her way to Seville, the center of commercial activity for the Americas, and to its port, Sanlúcar, and from there across the Atlantic to Punta de Araya.

This sequence suggests that Catalina was in some sense a good daughter, driven by a hunger for freedom but loathe to acknowledge, even to herself, what might well pain or disgrace her family. It seems clear that, for Catalina, to disguise herself as a man was to gain freedom from all daughterly responsibility, a freedom marked by her pious mother's failure to recognize her. On the subject of motivation, however, she is conspicuously silent, even evasive. The endless drama of inner life, so much a fixture of our present literature, is absent from her memoir, and we are left to infer, by a word here, a detail there, above all by the actions which shape her character, an ardent wish to escape the obligations of Spanish womanhood.

Elsewhere, and with equal circumspection, Catalina makes plain that the cost of that escape was a deep loss—of family, of community, of a sense of belonging. Her disguise made strangers of her own kin, who seem to crop up everywhere in the first chapter, and eventually drove her to kill her brother and to seek refuge time and again in the Church she had once fled. In the name of freedom, she lived a paradox and, as for so many citizens of the New World, her paradise of footloose anonymity threatened at every moment to become a boneyard of violence and disconnection—or worse, to seem altogether unpeopled.

Nowhere is this clearer than in the sequence of events in chapters 6 and 7, which deal with her brother Miguel and the aftermath of their fatal duel. When she first meets him in Concepción, Catalina's delight seems entirely genuine, and we are not surprised that she chooses to spend three years under his command, an unknown sister. But her disguise, as well as her liking for her brother's mistress, eventually brings them to blows, and while it all ends peacefully, the brawl results in Catalina's banishment to the Chilean front, to Paicabí ("a soldier's worst nightmare"), to Nacimiento ("a shortcut to the grave"), and to the Valley of Puren, scene of one of the bloodiest battles of the Araucanian Wars.

The fight also presages their fatal meeting several years later when, with typical indirection, Catalina accidentally kills her brother in another man's quarrel. Her handling of this disaster is particularly instructive. Chapter 6 ends with her terse expression of grief—"Captain Miguel de Erauso was dead, they buried him in the Franciscan monastery, and I watched from the choir—God knows in what misery!"—while chapter 7 opens with her trans-Andean flight to Tucumán across the dry, barren, body-strewn Cordillera. Ever the colonizer, Catalina rarely looks around her except to count churches and evaluate Peru's natural bounties, but in this, her most expansive moment of description, she conjures a vision of waste in which all the landscape conventions of medieval romance seem to reassert themselves. This passage gives way almost immediately to her finest comedy of disguise, as she eludes the marital designs of two different women. Notwithstanding the appeal to eros, however, we understand that Catalina's descent into outlawry has begun—chapter 7 ends with her stealing a mule—and that her life is now guided by remorse.

The third sequence of actions I wish to point to has to do with Catalina's sexual life. It is no surprise, given her circumspection in other areas, that Catalina is fairly mum when it comes to her sexual preferences. Only once is she explicit about her "taste . . . for pretty faces." Otherwise, from time to time, she twitches aside the curtain on a scene of unmistakable erotic activity, and we are left, without benefit of commentary, to piece things together. These scenes, scattered throughout her memoir, provide a delicious counterpoint to the principal narrative of male action and conquest, but they never coalesce into an independent plot of the sort we have come to expect when a heroine puts on breeches. Catalina's disguise falls, but within a plot driven by her increasing lawlessness and ill luck. Thus, there is no Shakespearean moment of gender recognition, no Sebastian to pronounce smugly that "nature to her bias drew," no disconsolate Phebe to exclaim, "If sight and shape be true, Why then, my love, adieu!"

The lack of a recognition scene of this sort is the unmistakable sign that Catalina's disguise transcends comic convention. However much it may delight us with the possibilities of transformation, the traditional comedy of cross-dressing is driven by the marriage plot, and as such strongly privileges heterosexuality, happily unknotting in the end all of the tangles which disguise has created. Such is not the case with Catalina's memoir. Though she was not above invoking certain comic conventions of the disguised heroine—especially when recounting how the attentions of other women threatened to lead to marriage—her story is free of the heterosexual bias that underlies such comedy. The men she portrays— whether masters, commanders, lawmen, troopmates, confessors, or gambling partners—are never potential lovers. The women, by contrast, almost always are. They range from young girls under the supervision of male guardians, to self-reliant wives and mistresses, to the cloistered nuns of Lima, Guamanga, and La Plata, and there is every reason to assume that some of them, at least, knew Catalina's secret.

While free of heterosexual bias, however, Catalina's memoir is not free of a certain contempt for other women which may strike some as male in flavor. Doña Beatriz de Cardenas's love of finery is ironically counterpointed by her closet lechery. Doña María Dávalos, the damsel in distress, is an unlooked-for bother whom Catalina willingly hands off to her mother, the La Plata nun. The women of Tucumán have no more sense than to plot marriage to the first young Spaniard to present "himself." There is a strong suggestion in these and other moments that Catalina's contempt is founded on a genuine disgust with the dependency and deception heterosexuality enjoins upon women.

But just as Catalina's cross-dressing is something other than a comic disguise, so her contempt for other women's heterosexual inclinations is something other than a simple disgust with the roles they must play in order to get and keep a man. Her preference for male clothing was absolute. It not only freed her from womanly obligations, sexual and otherwise, it also allowed her a freedom, sexual and otherwise, in the world at large. Long after that world had come to know who she was, she continued to dress as a man—with the pope's blessing, her male garb ceased to be a disguise and became a privilege.

The plot (if we may call it that) centering on Catalina's homosexual preferences is fractured, partial—not surprisingly in an autobiographical text that is now nearly four hundred years old—a sort of understory to the more visible narrative architecture of male conquest and aggression. It is never entirely out of sight, however, and surfaces with astonishing clarity and completeness in the final scene, when two Neapolitan prostitutes, engaged in turning a trick, pause momentarily to salute Catalina. This, the memoir's only true recognition scene, is at the same time, significantly, a scene of seduction. The prostitutes know Catalina, they beckon her in a lisping sing-song: "Señora Catalina, where are you going, all by your lonesome?" The question is full of sexual interest—who knows what Catalina's answer might have been, had she not interrupted them in the age-old pose of plying the opposite sex? Thus caught, however, they supply the final strokes to her self-portrait. With an outburst of conspicuously manly language, she silences their laughter and ends her story: "I have come to deliver one hundred strokes to your pretty little necks, and a hundred gashes with this blade to the fool who would defend your honor."

Are we justified in reading this final flourish of bravado as Catalina's parody of masculinist culture, with its vaunting claims of superior strength and its penchant for settling matters through physical action? Surely we are, and yet to see her simply as an indicter of male-dominated culture, an early feminist woman warrior come to set the record straight, is to sell short the complexity of Catalina's story. Throughout the memoir, Catalina has persistently made fun of men who talk big, only to find themselves bested by her in combat. From Señor Reyes in chapter 3 to the chatty Italian of chapter 25, she has exposed them as unskillful braggarts whose verbal insults to her "manhood" she is more than able to avenge. Conversely, her most fearsome opponent is the man she calls The Cid, a sinister figure in large part because he is a man of so few words. But while mere verbal machismo is always suspect in Catalina's eye, she never undercuts true skill in a soldier or swordsman—especially her own, of which she was justifiably proud. As Stephanie Merrim has written, "For women warriors such as Erauso, the mere change of dress effected a com-

plete change in gender identity."[4] The unveiled Catalina ex
ploits her "true" gender in shaping the story of her life, using
it to create moments of comedy and suspense, but her values
remain largely those of the men with whom she soldiered,
gambled, and fought.

Thus, while Catalina mocks her male opponents and the
heterosexual, hierarchical society to which they belong, she
also works to reaffirm that society, measuring her own accom-
plishments (and the validity of her own extraordinary narrative!) by the standards it sets forth. There is never a hint of
complaint, nary a plea that the reader regard her as "victim."
On the contrary, Catalina seeks only "to win," and her boast
is that she can do so, whatever the rules may be and whoever
may own them. Moreover, Catalina's victories—her sense of
self and valor—are culled from the land at the expense of the
indigenous people of the Indies, and often at the expense of
the women, Spanish-born or indigenous, whom she chances
upon during her travels. It would be a misreading to see her
as anything other than the perfect colonialist, manipulative,
grasping, and at moments out and out bigoted. To align Catalina, as a cross-dressing "other," with the victims of colonial-
ism is to miss the truth that the rewards of her transformation
were gained almost wholly at their expense.

At once racy and mordantly sarcastic, at times bitter, at
others bright, Catalina's memoir is as contradictory as the
New World itself. She is an anti-hero we can't help but like,
and yet regardless of how much we may like her, regardless of
her tongue-in-cheek criticisms of the subordinating masculinist culture, she is not one on whom we can easily hang a

4. Stephanie Merrim, "Catalina de Erauso: Prodigy of the Baroque Age," *Review:
Latin American Literature and Arts*, no. 43 (1990), p. 38.

sign or banner. A transvestite with passions, intelligence, and innate skill, Catalina de Erauso is also a colonialist, and in her version of new world history the underdog eagerly exchanges roles with those in power and, having gained power, exercises it just as capriciously. As a bizarre subtext to the colonialist tale of battlefield valor and bravery, Catalina's story reminds us that it is the invisible characters, hovering in obscurity about the edges of the scene, who complicate and thus complete the historical record. Today, as feminism finds itself at a crossroads, struggling with a crisis of identity, Catalina's strange and contradictory narrative may serve to illumine both the costs and the pleasures of independence in a changing, but still power-driven, society.

The little that is known of Catalina's life after 1626 exists in a handful of scattered documents. On September 29, 1629, in San Sebastian, she formally signed over to her married sister, Mariana, her portion of the family estate "as one of the children of Miguel de Erauso and María Pérez de Galarraga," receiving in exchange one thousand *reales* ready money and letters of credit to be redeemed in Madrid and Seville.[5] Then in 1630, she returned to the Americas, this time to Mexico, to live out the rest of her years there as Antonio de Erauso, mule-driver and small merchant.

We know this from two eyewitness accounts of Catalina in her later years, and they are worth quoting at length as the

5. Lucas G. Castillo Lara, *La Asombrosa historia de Doña Catalina de Erauso, La Monja Alférez, y sus Prodigiosas Aventuras en Indias* (Caracas: Editorial Planeta Venezolana, 1992), p. 318.

only such documents in existence. The first comes from Captain Juan Pérez de Aguirre, who testified in San Sebastian in 1640, in a hearing on the Erauso estate, that he had been

in the city of New Veracruz, in the Kingdom of New Spain, in March of 1639, and had asked Captain Domingo de Portu, of San Sebastian, and Captain Francisco de Endara, also of San Sebastian, for news of Miguel, Francisco, Martin and Domingo de Erauso, and had been told they were all dead—Francisco in the city of Lima, in his capacity as majordomo or secretary to the Viceroy; Miguel in Chile; and that he couldn't remember where the others were said to have died, but it was common knowledge that they were all dead, all excepting a brother [*hermano*] of theirs called *Don Antonio de Erauso, alias Alférez Monja*, with whom he had spoken at this same time, in the city of Veracruz, and who had confirmed the deaths of the four brothers.[6]

The second comes from Nicolás de la Rentería, who in 1693 dictated an account of his meeting with Catalina to a fellow Capuchin friar, declaring that, in 1645 in Veracruz,

he saw and spoke several times with La Monja Alférez doña Catarina de Erauso (who went there by the name of Antonio de Erauso); that she had a mule pack with which she, along with some slaves, carried stuff all over, and that on those mules and with the help of those slaves, she transported goods to Mexico; that she was the King's subject and known as a person of much courage and skill; that she went in men's clothing, and wore a sword and dagger orna-

6. Ibid., p. 322.

mented in silver. She seemed to be about fifty years old, of strong build, somewhat stout, swarthy in complexion, with a few hairs on her chin.[7]

A "Relación" of Catalina's final years, published in Mexico in 1653, places her death in 1650 in Orizava, on the road to Veracruz. She died an "exemplary death," according to the "Relación," and her funeral "was attended by the most important people of the town, for she had been loved by all of the nuns and priests in the region, and they gave her a sumptuous requiem and an honored sepulchre."[8]

This brief account is of doubtful authenticity, however, and may be an early example of the expurgative tradition that would soon transform Catalina into a legend of piety and penitence. Those pages in the Orizava church records for 1650, in which this event would have been noted, are mysteriously missing. The "honored sepulchre" where Catalina now rests has never been found.

MICHELE STEPTO
New Haven, 1995

7. Ibid., pp. 322–23.
8. Rima de Vallbona, ed., *Vida i Sucesos de la Monja Alférez* (Tempe, Arizona: Arizona State University, 1992), p. 174.

TRANSLATORS' NOTE

While the story of Catalina's life flourished in folklore, legend, drama, and other forms, the manuscript of her memoir led a quiet, unpublished existence. For a century or more following its composition, it was in the possession of the Urbizu family of Seville, the same family whose ancestor, Juan de Urquiza, had been Catalina's first master in Peru. Sometime during the eighteenth century, the Spanish poet Cándido María Trigueros made a copy of the original. From this copy, in 1784, the royal historian don Juan Bautista Muñoz (who may also have had access to the Seville original) made another copy. After Hispanicizing the Basque names and supplying a new title, *Vida y sucesos de la Monja Alférez . . . Escrita por ella misma,* Muñoz entered it in the papers for his *Historia del Nuevo Mundo,* which remained unpublished at his death. Sometime in the 1820s, the Basque gentleman Joaquin de Ferrer obtained a copy of the Muñoz *Vida y sucesos* and set about verifying most of the facts and dates recorded, and restoring the Basque spelling of many of the surnames. Finally, in 1829, Ferrer had the memoir printed in Paris for the first time, as *Historia de la Monja Alférez Doña Catalina de Erauso, escrita por ella misma—The Story of the Lieutenant Nun Doña Catalina de Erauso, written by herself.* Only the Muñoz and Ferrer copies of the original manuscript now exist. The present translation into English is based largely on a 1918 edition of Ferrer's *Historia,* though we have also consulted Muñoz's *Vida y sucesos*, recently made available in an excellent edition edited by Rima de Vallbona.

There are several challenges facing the translator who would render Catalina's memoir in English. One, at least, is insurmountable—there is no English equivalent for the gender inflections of the Spanish adjective, which make a primary, grammatical notation of gender with practically every sentence, thus setting up a drumbeat of sexual self-identification that reverberates from one end of the text to the other. The fact that Catalina almost invariably uses masculine endings to describe herself is lost in English, as are those rare moments when she chooses a feminine ending. The relative disconnectedness of the participial phrase in Spanish poses another grammatical problem. Catalina uses this disconnectedness to great effect in the erotic scene in chapter 5, where she substitutes the combined participial/indirect object for the plainer subject-verb coordination in a series of phrases that leave us dazzled and uncertain about the precise event being recorded: "Y un día, estando en el estrado *peinándome* acostado en sus faldas y *andándole* en las piernas . . . " (italics added). The playfulness here is inscribed in the Spanish grammar itself, and while that effect is not possible to reproduce in English (in good English, at least), the combined evasiveness and breathlessness may be achieved in other, chiefly rhythmic, ways.

Grammatical differences aside, there is the matter of Catalina's deadpan tonality, especially as regards religious and political institutions and rituals. While her memoir in many ways offers a psychological blueprint of the Spanish mentality of conquest, she is by no means without attitude toward the people and institutions that threaten her freedom in the kingdom of Peru. Often, she conveys that attitude by means of the list, yoking together item after item so as to suggest boredom, if not outright contempt. Fortunately, the list in English often produces the same effect—and this is especially true in American English, which, like other New World languages, has been shaped by the need to amass detail, whether in a spirit of wonder, or outrage, or sarcastic disbelief.

Finally, there is the question of how to convey the tremendous speed of Catalina's memoir, its tumbling rhythms, its actions piled upon actions, without either doing violence to the English sentence or lessening the energy of her narrative voice. It has helped to remember that Catalina may have dictated her memoirs to an amanuensis, perhaps as she paced up and down in some Seville parlor, waiting for permission from the Council on the Indies to return to the Americas—recounting with spirited delight the story of her adventures there, now and then lunging with an imaginary sword at some remembered opponent, perhaps frightening the hapless scribe who was setting down her words, and taking pleasure in that—and that for this reason the flavor of speech, which is not always careful or concise and which often repeats itself, permeates the inmost fabric of the narrative. With this in mind, we have relied heavily on colloquial American speech, with its bias toward storytelling, its homespun vocabulary, its winking metaphors, its love of "and" splices. Sometimes, colloquial American English has provided us with a surprisingly exact translation of Catalina's seventeenth-century Spanish, while other times it has captured, in our view, the spirit of her phrasing. Remembering also that Catalina's Peru was on the western frontier of Spain's New World empire, we have plumped for colloquialisms with a distinctly "Western" ring—readers familiar with Mark Twain's Huck Finn will detect his inspiring presence from time to time in this re creation of Catalina's voice.

All this aside, however, it has always seemed to us that the best translations were those that hued most closely to the original text, as opposed to those that take liberties with it in the name of invention or clarification. For this reason, nothing has been added here, nothing left out—not even the baffling discrepancies that dot the original.

LIEUTENANT NUN

CHAPTER 1

Her country, parents, nativity, education,
flight, and travels in various parts of Spain.

I, *doña Catalina de Erauso*, was born in the town of San
Sebastian in Guipúzcoa province, in the year 1585. My parents, Captain don Miguel de Erauso and doña María Pérez de
Galarraga y Arce, were native-born residents of the town,
and they raised me at home with my brothers and sisters until
I was four. In 1589, they placed me in a convent of Dominican
nuns there in town, San Sebastian the Elder, with my aunt
doña Ursula Unzá y Sarasti, who was my mother's older sister
and the prioress of the convent. There I lived until the age of
fifteen, in training for the day when I would profess myself a
nun.

In the year of my novitiate, toward the end of it, when I
was about to make my final vows, I got in a quarrel with one
of the sisters, doña Catalina de Aliri, who had entered the
convent and taken the veil after the death of her husband.
She was a big, robust woman, I was but a girl—and when she
beat me, I felt it. It was on Saint Joseph's eve, March 18,
1600, when the entire convent rose at midnight to perform
matins, that I went into the choir and found my aunt on her
knees. She called me over, handed me the key to her cell and
asked me to fetch her breviary. I went after it, unlocked her
cell door and grabbed up the breviary, and seeing the keys to

the convent dangling from a nail on the wall, I left the cell open and returned the key and the breviary to my aunt.

The nuns were singing the psalms in a mournful tone, and when they got to the first lesson I went to my aunt and asked to be excused, telling her I was sick. She touched her hand to my forehead and said, "Go on, go to bed." I left the choir, took up a lamp and returned to my aunt's cell. I took a pair of scissors and a needle and thread, I took some of the pieces of eight that were lying there, and the keys to the convent, and I left. I went opening doors and closing them carefully behind me, and when I came to the last one I shook off my veil and went out into a street I had never seen, without any idea which way to turn, or where I might be going. I struck out, in what direction I cannot say, and came upon a chestnut grove just beyond the walls, on the outskirts of the convent grounds. There, I holed up for three days, planning and re-planning and cutting myself out a suit of clothes. With the blue woollen bodice I had I made a pair of breeches, and with the green petticoat I wore underneath, a doublet and hose—my nun's habit was useless and I threw it away, I cut my hair and threw it away, and on the third night, wanting to get as far from that place as I possibly could, I set off without knowing where I was going, threading my way down roads and passing villages, until I came to the town of Vitoria, some twenty leagues from San Sebastian, on foot, tired, and having eaten nothing more than the herbs I had found growing by the roadside.

I entered Vitoria without the least idea where to put up, but it wasn't more than a few days before I met a certain doctor of theology, don Francisco de Cerralta, who took me in without any fuss, despite the fact that he didn't know me, and even gave me some new clothes. He was married, as I soon discovered, to yet another of my mother's sisters, but I didn't let on as to who I was. I stayed there what must have been three months, and the doctor, seeing that I read Latin well, took a fancy to me and got the idea in his head I should continue my training as his student. When I let him know I wasn't interested, he pleaded and insisted and finally went so far as to lay his hands on me.

With this, I decided to leave—and that is exactly what I did. I relieved him of some few *cuartos* I found lying about the place, and when I found a driver headed for Valladolid, I struck a deal for twelve *reales* and set out with him for that city, which is about forty-five leagues away.

The Court was in Valladolid at the time, and it wasn't long before I found work as a page with the king's secretary, don Juan de Idiáquez, who immediately dressed me up in a fine new set of clothes. There I went by the name of Francisco Loyola, and for seven months I did very well for myself. But at the end of that time, one evening when I was standing in the gate with one of the other pages, who should arrive but my father, asking whether Señor don Juan was at home. My friend responded yes, the don was at home, and my father told him to tell the don he was there. The other page went inside and I was left there with my father. The two of us didn't speak a word to each other, nor did he recognize me, and when my friend returned to say he might go in, my father started up the stairs, with me following along behind him.

Don Juan met him at the top of the stairs, embraced him warmly, and exclaimed, "Señor Captain, how good of you to visit!" From the way my father answered, the don could tell there was some trouble, and dismissing the person he had been seeing he came back and sat down with my father and asked him what the story was. My father explained how his daughter had run away from the convent, how he had searched high and low for her, and how it was this very thing that brought him to Valladolid. Don Juan showed his deep concern on account of the grief it caused my father, and his own fondness for me as well—and there were other things too, the matter of the convent, which his ancestors had founded and of which he was now a patron, and the town itself, of which he was also a native.

I had listened in on the conversation, and when I heard the anguish in my father's voice, I backed off slowly and slipped away to my room. I got my clothes and some eight doubloons I had squirreled away and made my way to an inn, where I slept that night, and caught wind of a driver leaving the next morning for Bilbao. I settled on a price with the man and left the next day, with no better idea of where to go, or what to do, than let myself be carried off like a feather in the wind.

It was a long road to Bilbao, some forty leagues I imagine, and at the end of it I could find neither inn nor private lodging, and was at my wit's end. Before long, I managed to attract the attention of some of the town's youths, who encircled me, edging up closer and closer, until finally I had had enough and picked up some stones and let one of them have it—where I cannot say, because I didn't see. I was arrested and thrown in jail, and there I remained for one long month, until the boy I had hit got better and I was set free, my pockets several *cuartos* lighter for the cost of my stay.

From Bilbao, just as soon as I was let go, I headed for Estella in the province of Navarre, which must be about twenty leagues off. I found work there as page to don Carlos de Arellano, a native of Santiago, and remained in his house and employment for two years, well-fed and well-clothed. But at the end of that time, with no more reason than that it suited me, I quit the comfort of this situation and returned to my hometown of San Sebastian, ten leagues away, where I remained completely unrecognized, a well-dressed young bachelor

One day, I went to hear mass at my old convent, the same mass my mother attended, and I saw that when she looked at me she did not recognize me, and when the mass was over and some of the nuns beckoned me into the choir, I made like I didn't understand, and with a bow here and a fine word there slipped out the door. This would have been at the beginning of the year 1603.

From San Sebastian I traveled to the port of Pasajes, a league away, and there stumbled upon one Captain Miguel de Berroiz, who was about to embark for Seville. I asked the man to take me with him, we settled on a price of forty *reales*, I went on board, we set sail, and before long arrived in Sanlúcar. I disembarked and went off to see Seville, and though I liked the place and thought about staying on for a while, in the end I was only there for two days, and then returned to Sanlúcar. There I met up with a Captain Miguel de Echarreta, a native of my own province. His ship was escorting the galleons of General don Luis Fernández de Córdoba, part of the Royal Armada which set sail for Punta de Araya in 1603 under the command of don Luis Fajardo, and I found work as ship's boy on the galleon of my uncle, Captain Esteban Eguiño, a first cousin to my mother who now lives in San Sebastian.

I went on board, and we set sail from Sanlúcar on Holy Monday in the year 1603.

CHAPTER 2

The departure from Sanlúcar for Punta de Araya,
Cartagena, Nombre de Dios, and Panama.

The work was new to me and I had a hard time of it at first. My uncle, with no idea who I was, grew fond of me and took me under his wing, especially when he heard where I was from and the names of my parents, which I concocted for him. When we reached Punta de Araya, we encountered a flotilla of enemy ships holding the coast, and our fleet drove them off. Finally, we arrived in Cartagena of the Indies, and there we remained for eight days. I signed off as ship's boy and became my uncle Captain Eguiño's cabinboy. From Cartagena we sailed on to Nombre de Dios and remained there for nine days, and during that time many of our men died, which put us in a great hurry to be on our way again.

Once the silver had been loaded on the ship and everything made ready for the return voyage to Spain, I dealt my uncle a heavy blow, helping myself to five hundred of his *pesos*. That night at about ten, while my uncle was sleeping, I left the cabin and told the guards the captain was sending me ashore on business. Seeing as how they knew me, they easily let me pass, I leapt ashore, and that was the last they ever saw of me. An hour later, the ship had weighed anchor and set sail.

Once the rest of the fleet had departed, I found work with a certain Captain Juan de Ibarra, the treasury agent for Panama, who is still alive, and five or six days later we departed for Panama, where he was living at the time, and I stayed on with him there for some three months. He wasn't a particularly generous man and the little he gave me was soon gone, as well as whatever I had pilfered from my uncle, all spent, so that now I was penniless, and I set off to look for a living elsewhere.

After much asking around, I heard of a Trujillan merchant, one Juan de Urquiza, and I signed on with him and did very well for myself the three months we were together in Panama.

CHAPTER 3

From Panama she travels with her new master,
Urquiza, the Trujillan merchant, to the port
of Paita and the village of Saña.

I *left Panama* with my new master, Juan de Urquiza, aboard a frigate bound for the port of Paita, where he was expecting a large shipment. But as we neared the port of Manta, we were overtaken by such foul weather that the ship capsized in a squall, and those who could swim—myself, my master, and some others—made it to shore. All the rest drowned. In Manta, we managed to find passage on one of the king's galleons, for a princely sum, and we headed for the port of Paita, where my master found his shipment as expected in a vessel belonging to a Captain Alonso Cerrato. He then charged me with the task of sending on the shipment in numerical order, and went on ahead.

I set myself to the task I had been given, unloading the goods and sending them on in the proper order. All the while my master was receiving the stuff in Saña, some sixty leagues away, and when I had finished unloading everything, I set out from Paita with the last few items to rejoin him.

When I arrived in Saña, my master gave me a warm welcome, delighted with the work I had done and with the deal itself, and straightaway he gave me two new outfits, one black and the other brightly colored. He set me up in one of his shops, placing in my care a great deal of property in the form of both goods and cash, all in all more than one hundred and thirty thousand *pesos'* worth, and then he wrote down in a book the various prices of the items and how I was to sell them. He left two slaves to assist me, and a black woman who was to cook for me, and indicated I was to spend three *pesos* on daily expenses, and having done this, he loaded up the rest of the goods and took them on to Trujillo, some thirty-two leagues away.

Now, in this book I've just mentioned, my master also left the names of the people I could trust to take goods on credit, provided I did so carefully, with my wits about me, and made a note of each sale in the book. In particular, he wanted me to know that this applied to my lady doña Beatriz de Cárdenas, whom he held in perfect confidence and high regard. My master then left for Trujillo, and I remained behind in the shop in Saña, selling the goods according to the guidelines he had given me, collecting the money, and making notes in the book as to the day, month, and year of the sale, the item, the quantity, the name of the customer, and the prices—and doing the same with all of the purchases on credit.

Immediately, my lady doña Beatriz de Cárdenas began taking goods, and went on taking so much, and for so long, that I began to have my doubts—and without letting her know what I was up to, I wrote my master in Trujillo telling him in detail about the whole affair. He wrote back that that was perfectly all right, and that, so far as the lady's penchant was concerned, even if she asked me for the entire shop, I should give it to her. So I put the letter safely away, and carried on with business as usual.

Who would have guessed those tranquil days were numbered, or that trouble lay just around the next corner! One

Sunday, when I had gone to the theater and pulled up a chair to enjoy the show, a certain Reyes showed up, and placed his chair squarely in front of mine, and so close up I couldn't see a thing—I asked him if he wouldn't mind moving a bit to the side, he responded in a nasty tone, and I gave him back a little of the same. Then he told me I'd best disappear, or he'd be forced to cut my face wide open. Seeing as how I was weaponless, except for a short dagger, I made my exit, more than a little enraged, and with a couple of friends at my side who followed along trying to calm me down.

The next morning, a Monday, I was in the shop doing business as usual when I saw Reyes walk past the door, first one way and then the other. I closed the shop, grabbed up a knife, and went looking for a barber to grind the blade to a sawtoothed edge, and then, throwing on my sword—it was the first I ever wore—I went looking for Reyes and found him where he was strolling by the church with a friend.

I approached him from behind and said, "Ah, señor Reyes!"

He turned and asked, "What do you want?"

I said, "This is the face you were thinking of cutting up," and gave him a slash worth ten stitches.

He clutched at the wound with both hands, his friend drew his sword and came at me, and I went at him with my own. We met, I thrust the blade through his left side, and down he went.

I ran straight into the church, followed just as quickly by the sheriff, don Mendo de Quiñones, a knight of Alcántara, who dragged me out and carted me off to jail—the first I was ever in—and clapped me in irons and threw me in a cell. I got word to my master, thirty-two leagues off in Trujillo, and he came at once and spoke to the sheriff and, by dint of one thing or another, managed to get the irons removed. He continued to plead my case and I was returned to the church, and three months later, after numerous appeals and maneuvers on the part of the head bishop, I was free to go.

At this point, my master told me he had figured out a way for me to get out of this mess without the law banishing me, or Reyes or one of his friends killing me, and it was this—I should marry doña Beatriz de Cárdenas, whose niece was married to that no-good Reyes himself, whose face I had cut up. Do this, he said, and everything would calm down.

Now, it should be noted that doña Beatriz de Cárdenas was my master's mistress, and that what he had in mind was to hold on to the both of us—me for business and her for pleasure. And they must have worked the whole thing out between them, because after I had been taken back to the church I used to sneak out at night to the lady's house, and there she would caress me, and implore me, supposedly for fear of the law, not to go back to the church but to stay with her. Finally one night, she locked me in and declared that come hell or high water I was going to sleep with her—pushing and pleading so much that I had to smack her one and slip out of there.

I lost no time in telling my master this marriage just wasn't going to happen, that there wasn't any way in the world I was going to have a thing to do with it. He begged and pleaded and promised me mountains of gold, reminding me of the lady's beauty and talents, and how this would put an end to all that business with Reyes, and he mentioned other things too—still, I held my ground.

Once he saw this was the case, he said I should go to Trujillo and set up shop there—and that is exactly what I did.

CHAPTER 4

She leaves Saña for Trujillo
and there murders a man.

I *moved on to the city* of Trujillo, which is under the authority of the bishop of Lima, where my master had set up a shop for me. I started to work, conducting business just as I had in Saña, with another book like the one I had used there, containing information about the stock, the prices, and the accounts on credit.

It must have been about two months later, one morning around eight, as I was cashing one of my master's notes for some twenty-four thousand *pesos*, a Negro came in and told me there were some men at the door who appeared to be armed. This put me on guard. I woke the accountant, got my receipt, and sent word for Francisco Zerain, who came directly and as he entered the shop recognized the three men as Reyes, the friend of his I had run through in Saña, and another man.

I told the Negro to close the door, Zerain and I went outside, and at once they threw themselves upon us. We met them fighting, and it wasn't long before, as my bad luck would have it, I ran my sword point through Reyes' friend—where, I cannot say—and down he went. And so with blood drawn on both sides, we went on fighting, two on two.

At this moment the sheriff don Ordoño de Aguirre arrived,

together with two of his deputies, and they grabbed hold of me. Francisco Zerain took to his heels and managed to escape. The choriff took personal charge of me, leaving his deputies to take care of the others, and as we were walking toward the jail he asked me who I was and where I was from, and when I told him I was a Basquero, he said to me in Basque that when we came to the cathedral I might consider loosening the belt he was holding me by. I took the hint, did exactly as he said, and darted into the cathedral while he stood outside bellowing for help.

Once inside, I sent word to my master in Saña. He arrived shortly thereafter and tried to settle the matter, but he made no headway because in addition to murder they had charged me with God knows what else, and the only way out of the whole mess, it seemed, was for me to slip off to Lima.

I turned in my books, my master furnished me with two suits of clothing, two thousand six hundred pesos, a letter of introduction—and off I went.

CHAPTER 5

From Trujillo to Lima.

With *Trujillo behind me*, and having traveled more than eighty leagues, I came to the city of Lima, capital of the opulent kingdom of Peru, which includes a hundred and two Spanish cities, not to mention many towns and villages, twenty-eight bishophrics and archbishophrics, a hundred and thirty-six sheriffs, and the Royal Courts of Valladolid, Granada, Charcas, Quito, Chile, and La Paz. The city of Lima has an archbishop and a cathedral, much like the one in Seville (though not as large), five benefices, ten canons, six whole and six half prebends, four priests, seven parishes, twelve convents of friars and nuns, eight hospitals, a hermitage (of the Inquisition—the other is in Cartagena), a university. . . . It also has the viceroy and the Royal Court which govern the rest of Peru, and many other splendors.

At my master's bidding, I presented the letter to Diego de Solarte, a wealthy merchant who today is the chief consul in Lima. He received me in his house in a most kind and gracious manner, and a couple of days later put me in charge of his shop, with a yearly salary of six hundred *pesos*, and there I worked, much to his satisfaction and content.

But at the end of nine months, he told me I should think about making my living elsewhere, the reason being that there were two young ladies in the house, his wife's sisters, and I had become accustomed to frolicking with them and teasing them one, in particular, who had taken a fancy to me. And one day, when she and I were in the front parlor, and I had my head in the folds of her skirt and she was combing my hair while I ran my hand up and down between her legs, Diego de Solarte happened to pass by the window, and spied us through the grate, just as she was telling me I should go to Potosí and seek my fortune, so that the two of us could be married. Solarte went to his office, called for me a little while later, asked for the books, took them, fired me, and I left.

I found myself in a sticky spot, with no work and no friends. At that time in Lima, they were raising six companies to fight in Chile, and I joined one, signing on as a soldier, and immediately received the allotted salary of two hundred and eighty *pesos*. When my master found out, he took it very hard. Apparently, this was not exactly what he had in mind. He offered to speak to the company officers and get my enlistment annulled and to repay the money they had given me—but I wasn't interested and I told him so, I had a mind to travel and see a bit of the world.

And so, assigned to the company of Captain Gonzalo Rodríguez, I left Lima in a troop of one thousand six hundred men under the command of the fieldmaster Bravo de Sarabia, on the way to the city of Concepción, some five hundred and forty leagues off.

CHAPTER 6

She arrives in Concepción in Chile and there
encounters her brother. She moves on to
Paicabí, where she takes part in the battle
of Valdivia, rescuing the company colors.
She returns to Concepción, kills two men
and her own brother.

After twenty days at sea, we came to the port of Concepción, a decent-sized town that goes by the nickname *the noble and the loyal,* and has its own bishop. Troops were scarce in Chile at the time and our arrival was welcome, and we received immediate orders to disembark. They came from the governor, Alonso de Ribera, conveyed by his secretary, Captain Miguel de Erauso. As soon as I heard the name I was overjoyed, and I knew it was my brother, because while I didn't know him—indeed, had never laid eyes on him because he left San Sebastian when I was only two—I had had news of him even if I didn't know his exact whereabouts. He took the roll book and went walking up and down the line, asking each of us our names and where we were from, and when he came to me and heard my name and my country, he dropped his pen, threw his arms around me, and asked for news of his father and mother, his brothers and sisters, and his beloved Catalina, the nun. I responded as best I could without giving myself away or rousing his suspicions.

And so he went on with the roll call, and when he had finished he invited me to have supper at his house and we sat down to eat. He told me that the garrison we were assigned to at Paicabí was a soldier's worst nightmare, and that he would talk to the governor to see if he couldn't get me a new post. And at one point during the meal, he went up to see the governor, taking me with him, reported to him the arrival of the new recruits, and begged him as a favor to reassign to his company a certain young greenhorn from his own province, saying he hadn't seen any of his own countrymen since leaving home. The governor had me brought in, and when he saw me—I cannot say why—he said there was nothing he could do. My brother was crushed and left the room, but then a little while later the governor called him back and told him it should be as he requested.

So that, when the companies marched out, I stayed behind as my brother's soldier, and dined at his table for three years, all the while never letting on to my secret. On occasion, I went with him to the house of the mistress he kept in town, and on other occasions I went there without him. It wasn't long before he found out and, imagining the worst, he told me that he'd better not catch me at it again. But he spied on me, and when he caught me there the next time he waited outside, and when I came out he lit into me with his belt, wounding me in the hand.

I was forced to defend myself, and the sound of our brawling brought the Captain Francisco de Aillón, and he made peace between us. Still, for fear of the governor, who was a stickler for rules, I had to take refuge in the church of San Francisco, and there I remained, even though my brother interceded on my behalf, until the day he came to tell me I had been banished to Paicabí. There was nothing to be done, I was forced to leave for Paicabí, where I remained for three years.

So there I was, in Paicabí, for three years of misery, and after having always led the good life. What with the swarms of Indians in those parts, we ate, drank, and slept in our armor, until finally the governor, Alonso de Sarabia, arrived with the rest of the armies of Chile. We joined up with them and were quartered in the plains of Valdivia, on open ground, five thousand men, with everything but discomfort in short supply. The Indians sacked Valdivia and took the field. Three or four times before, we had marched out to meet them and engaged them on the field, always gaining the upper hand and butchering them—but in the last battle reinforcements arrived and it went badly for us, and they killed many of our men, captains, my own lieutenant, and rode off with the company flag.

When I saw the flag being carried off I rode after it, with two horsemen at my side, through the midst of a great multitude of Indians, trampling and slashing away and taking some wounds in return. Before long, one of the three of us fell dead, and the two that remained pressed on until we overtook the flag. But then my other companion went down, spitted on a lance. I had taken a bad blow to the leg, but I killed the chief who was carrying the flag, pulled it from his body and spurred my horse on, trampling and killing and slaughtering more men than there are numbers—but badly wounded, with three arrows in me and a gash from a lance in my left shoulder which had me in great pain—until at last I reached our own lines and fell from my horse. A few men came to my side, among them my brother, whom I hadn't seen in a while, and this was a great comfort to me. My wounds were tended to, and we stayed quartered there for nine months. At the end of that time, my brother brought me the flag I had rescued, a present from the governor, and I became the lieutenant of Alonso Moreno's company, which soon came under the command of Captain Gonzalo Rodríguez—the first captain I had ever served under—and all in all, I prospered and was well taken care of.

I served as a lieutenant for five years. I was there at the battle of Puren where my captain fell, leaving me in command of the company for some six months, and during that time I had a number of encounters with the enemy and took a few arrows. In one battle, I came up against one of the Indian captains, Francisco Quispiguaucha, a newly made Christian and a rich one too, whose devilish raids gave us plenty of trouble. I met him on the field, threw him from his horse, and he surrendered to me. I immediately strung him up from the nearest tree, and this made the governor furious, for as it turned out he had wanted the man taken alive, and they say it was for this reason he didn't give me the company, but gave it to Captain Casadevante instead, and put me on half-pay with some promising noises about next time.

The armies withdrew, each company back to its own garrison, and I went on to Nacimiento, which despite its fine name is nothing more than a shortcut to the grave—and there again I all but ate, drank, and slept in my armor. But I'd only been there a few days when fieldmaster Alvaro Núñez de Pineda arrived with orders from the governor to form a detachment for the Valley of Puren, some eight hundred cavalry from our garrison and others, and I was numbered among them, along with other officers and captains. We headed out for the Valley of Puren, and were on the rampage there for six months or so, slashing and burning Indian croplands. Later, the Governor

Alonso de Ribera gave me permission to go back to Concepción, and I returned to my post in the company of Francisco Navarette, and there I remained.

But Chance toyed with me, turning my every scrap of luck into disaster. I had been leading a quiet life in Concepción until, one day, when I was in the guard camp, I went into a nearby gambling house with a fellow lieutenant. We began to play and the game was going along smoothly, when a small misunderstanding came up and my companion, with plenty of people around to hear it, told me I lied like a cuckold. I drew out my dagger and ran it into his chest. So many people jumped on me—those at the table, and those that came running at the sound of the brawl—that I couldn't budge. One of the attachés held me fast until the local judge, Francisco de Párraga, came in, and he grabbed me tight as well and shook me this way and that, firing I don't know what questions at me. I told him that I would make my statement before the governor.

At this point, my brother came in and told me, in Basque, to run for my life. The judge grabbed me by my jacket collar and, dagger in hand, I told him to turn me loose—but the man shook me again, and I let him have it, slicing him across both cheeks—and still he held fast, so that I gave him another one, and he let go. I drew my sword as the whole room charged at me, backed toward the door, leveling whatever got in my way, and made my escape into a nearby Franciscan church, where I learned that both the lieutenant and the judge were dead.

This brought out the governor, Alonso García Remón, who had the church surrounded with soldiers and kept it that way for six months. He issued a proclamation, offering a reward to the man who took me alive, and forbidding my embarkation at any port. He alerted the various garrisons and market places—and took other precautions as well—until time, which cures all things, also cured his vigilance. Petitions on my behalf began to pile up, the guards surrounding the church were removed, the general air of alarm seemed to lift, and as I began to feel more at ease and even receive visits from friends, people began to talk about how provoked I had been in the first place, and what a tight spot I had been in.

One of the friends who came to see me during this time was don Juan de Silva, a full lieutenant, who told me he'd had some words with a certain don Francisco de Rojas, a knight of Santiago, and that he had challenged him to a duel for eleven that night. Each man was to bring a second, he said, and he had no one to turn to but myself.

I didn't answer at first, thinking it was some sort of trap. Juan de Silva guessed what was on my mind, and said, "If you're not with me, so be it, I will go alone. There is no other man I trust at my side." I said to myself, "What can you be thinking?" and accepted.

As the bells were ringing out for evening prayer, I left the church and went to his house. We dined and chatted about one thing or another until ten o'clock, when we heard the bells strike the hour and gathered up our swords and cloaks and set out for the spot. The darkness was so thick, you couldn't see your hand in front of your face—and noting this, I suggested we should tie our handkerchiefs around our arms so that, whatever might happen in the next couple of hours, we would not mistake one another.

The two men arrived, and one of them said, "Don Juan de Silva?" and I could tell by the voice it was don Francisco de Rojas.

Don Juan answered, "Here I am!" and they each laid hand to sword and went at each other, while the other man and I stood by.

They went on ducling, and after a while I could tell my friend had taken a hit and that he wasn't any the better for it. I jumped to his side and the other man took the side of don Francisco, we parried two on two, and before long don Francisco and don Juan fell to the ground. My opponent and I kept fighting, and my point went home below his left nipple, as I later learned, through what felt like a double thickness of leather, and he fell to the ground.

"Ah, traitor," he said, "you have killed me!" I thought I recognized this stranger's voice.

"Who are you?" I asked, and he answered, "Captain Miguel de Erauso."

I was stunned. My brother begged for a priest, as did the other two, and I went running to the Franciscan church and dispatched two friars to take their confessions. The other two died on the spot—and my brother was carried to the house of the governor, whom he had served as secretary of war. A doctor and a surgeon were summoned to tend to his wounds, and they did what they could. Then a statement was taken and they asked him the name of his murderer, and when my brother begged for a mouthful of wine, the doctor, whose name was Robledo, said no, it would not be advisable, and he begged again, and again the doctor refused, and my brother said, "Why, Sir, you are crueler to me than Lieutenant Díaz was!"—and after a few minutes, he passed away.

At this point, the governor had the church surrounded and tried to force his way in with his personal guard. The friars resisted, along with their superior, a certain brother Francisco de Otaloza who today lives in Lima, and a hot argument ensued, until a couple of the brothers plucked up their courage and told the governor to think it over carefully, because if he came in he could forget about leaving, and with that the governor cooled down and withdrew, leaving some guards behind.

Captain Miguel de Erauso was dead, they buried him in the Franciscan monastery, and I watched from the choir— God knows in what misery! I stayed there for eight months while they prosecuted me on a charge of rebellion—a charge I was given no opportunity to defend myself against.

When don Juan Ponce de León offered me his protection, I saw my chance. He gave me a horse and weapons and wished me godspeed out of Concepción, on to Valdivia and Tucumán.

CHAPTER 7

She leaves Concepción for Tucumán.

I *set out along the coast,* suffering a good deal, especially from thirst, for there was no fresh water to be had for miles around. Along the way, I fell in with two other soldiers, deserters both, and we continued on our way together, determined to die rather than let ourselves be arrested. We had our horses, our swords, our firearms, and the guidance of God on high. We ascended into the mountains, climbing for more than thirty leagues, and in all of them and the three hundred more we traveled, we didn't meet up with a single mouthful of bread, and only rarely some water or a clump of rough herbs, or some small animals, and now and then a gnarled root to keep us alive, and now and then an Indian who fled before us. We were forced to kill one of the horses and dry its meat, but we found that it was little more than skin and bones—and as we pressed onward, step by step, mile after mile, the others met the same fate, until we were left with only our feet to carry us and barely enough strength to stand.

The land grew cold—so cold we were half-frozen. One day from a distance we saw two men leaning against a rock and this gave us heart. We pushed on towards them, calling out as we came, asking what they were doing there, but they never answered. When we came to the spot, we saw they were dead—frozen through, their mouths hanging open as if they were laughing, and this filled us with terror.

We pressed on and three nights later, as we rested against a rock, one of the others gave out and died. The two of us went on and the next day, at about four in the afternoon, my companion dropped to the ground sobbing, unable to go another step, and he died. I found eight *pesos* in his pocket and pressed on blindly, clutching my rifle and the last scrap of dried meat, expecting any moment to share my companions' fate. You can imagine my wretched state, dead tired, barefoot, my feet in shreds. I propped myself against a tree and wept—for what I think was the first time in my life—I recited the rosary, commending myself to the Most Holy Virgin and to her husband, glorious Saint Joseph. I rested a little, got back on my feet, and began to walk again, and judging by the climate I must have walked clear out of the kingdom of Chile and into Tucumán.

I kept on going and the next morning, as I lay stretched out on the ground, overcome by fatigue and hunger, I caught sight of two men approaching on horseback. And I didn't know whether to rejoice or tremble—were they cannibals or Christians? I couldn't tell—and without even the strength to take aim, I loaded my rifle.

They rode up and asked me what I was doing in that godforsaken place, and I could see they were Christians, and the heavens seemed to open before me. I told them I was lost, that I didn't know where I was, that I was wracked with fatigue, dead with hunger, too weak to even stand. It pained them to see me like that and, dismounting, they gave me what food they had, loaded me up on one of the horses, and carried me to what they said was their mistress's ranch, some three leagues away, and we arrived there around five in the afternoon.

The lady was a half-breed, the daughter of a Spaniard and an Indian woman, a widow and a good woman. When she saw how broken and friendless I was, she took pity on me, gave me a decent bed to sleep in, a good meal, and told me to rest— after which, I felt much better. The next morning, she fed me well, and seeing as I was so entirely destitute she gave me a decent cloth suit, and went on treating me handsomely, making me small gifts of this and that. The lady was well-off, with a good deal of livestock and cattle, and it seems that, since Spaniards were scarce in those parts, she began to fancy me as a husband for her daughter.

After I'd been there for eight days, the good woman said she wanted me to stay on and manage the place. I let her know how grateful I was, seeing how I was penniless, and told her I would serve her to the best of my abilities. And a couple of days later, she let me know it would be fine by her if I married her daughter—a girl as black and ugly as the devil himself, quite the opposite of my taste, which has always run to pretty faces. Still, I pretended to be overcome with happiness—so much good fortune, and for one so undeserving!—and I threw myself at her feet, telling her I was hers to dispose of as she pleased, as one she had snatched from the jaws of ruin, and I went on serving her as well as I knew how.

The woman tricked me out like a dandy and gave me full run of the house and the lands. After two months, we went into Tucumán for the wedding, and there I remained for another two months, delaying the thing on one pretext or another until, finally, I couldn't take it anymore and I stole a mule and cleared out—and that was the last they ever saw of me.

It was during this time in Tucumán that I had another adventure of the same sort. In the two months while I was putting off the Indian woman, I struck up a casual friendship with the bishop's secretary, who made quite a fuss over me and more than once invited me to his house, where we played cards and where I met a certain churchman, don Antonio de Cervantes, the bishop's vicar-general. This gentleman also took a fancy to me, and gave me gifts and wined me and dined me at his house until, finally, he came to the point, and told me that he had a niece living with him who was just about my age, a girl of many charms, not to mention a fine dowry, and that he had a mind to see the two of us married—and so did she.

I pretended to be quite humbled by his flattering intentions. I met the girl, and she seemed good enough. She sent me a suit of good velvet, twelve shirts, six pairs of Rouen breeches, a collar of fine Dutch linen, a dozen handkerchiefs, and two hundred pesos in a silver dish—all of this a gift, sent simply as a compliment, and having nothing to do with the dowry itself.

Well, I received it all gratefully and composed the best thank-you I knew how, saying I was on fire for the moment when I would kiss her hand and throw myself at her feet. I hid as much of the stuff as I could from the Indian woman, and as for the rest I led her to believe it was a gift from don Antonio, something on the occasion of my marriage to her daughter, whom that gentleman had heard of and thought the world of—especially considering I was so crazy about her myself.

This is how things stood when I saddled up and vanished. And I have never heard exactly what became of the black girl or the little vicaress.

CHAPTER 8

From Tucumán to Potosí.

I *left Tucumán,* as I have said, and made my way to Potosí, some five hundred and fifty leagues away. It took me more than three months to cover the distance, crossing territory that was bitter cold and all but uninhabited.

A little ways out I fell in with a soldier going in the same direction, and I was glad for the company, and we continued together. A little further on and three men in caps, carrying shotguns, pounced upon us from behind some watering troughs along the side of the road and ordered us to hand over everything we had. There was no way to deter them from their enterprise, or convince them we didn't have a thing worth giving them—and so we were obliged to dismount and face them, with us shooting at them and they at us. They missed, and two of them fell dead—the third took off running—and we got back on our horses and continued on our way.

Finally, after three months of hard travel and several bad scrapes, we came to Potosí. Neither one of us knew a soul there and we parted ways, each to his own devices. I met up with Juan López de Arguijo, an alderman of the city of La Plata, in Charcas province, and found work with him as his *camarero* (or steward) at a fixed salary of nine hundred pesos a year. He put me in charge of twelve thousand head of llama and eighty Indians, and I left with them for Charcas, where my master was also bound. But shortly after we arrived, my master got himself mixed up in an unpleasant business with some men there in town, and the whole thing led to quarrels and hostages and the confiscation of property—at which point I decided to take my leave and retrace my steps to Potosí.

It wasn't very long after that the Alonso Ibáñez uprising occurred. The sheriff at the time was Rafael Ortiz, a knight of Santiago, and he raised more than a hundred men, myself included, to go up against the rebels. We went out to meet them one night in Santo Domingo street, and the sheriff shouted, "Who goes there?" at the top of his lungs. The rebels backed up without saying a word, and again he shouted, "Who goes there?"

"Liberty!" some of them shouted back.

Then the sheriff bellowed out, "Long live the King!" with many of the men echoing his words, and he charged toward them, with the rest of us right behind, stabbing and shooting. At that same instant, the rebels prepared to defend themselves, but we backed them into an alley and then came at them from behind around the other end, lashing away at them until they were forced to surrender.

Some had escaped but we arrested thirty-six, among them Ibáñez. We found seven of their men dead, and two of our own, with a pile of wounded on both sides. Some of those arrested were tortured and confessed that an uprising had been planned for that night. Three companies of Basqueros and men from up in the mountains were raised to defend the city, and after fifteen days all of the rebels had been hanged, and the city was quiet again.

At this time, because of some role I might have played in the uprising, or perhaps because of something I had done earlier, I was given the position of attaché to the sergeant major, a post I held for two years. While I was serving in Potosí, Governor Pedro de Legui of Santiago issued an order to raise soldiers for Chuncos and El Dorado, a region of hostile Indians some five hundred leagues from Potosí—and a land rich in gold and precious stones. Fieldmaster Bartolomé de Alba outfitted the expedition and plotted its route, and twenty days later, when everything was in order, we were marching out of Potosí.

CHAPTER 9

She leaves Potosí for Chuncos.

O_n *the road* from Potosí to Chuncos, we came upon a village of peaceful Indians called Arzaga, where we stayed for eight days. Here we took on guides for the journey, but we lost the way just the same, along with twelve men and fifty mules packed with supplies and ammunition, when we snarled up on some high rocks and they went over a cliff.

As we traveled inland, we discovered lush plains teeming with countless almond trees, like those in Spain, along with olive trees and other fruit. The governor got it in his head that we should plant crops here, in order to make up for what we had lost, but the infantry wouldn't go along with it, saying we didn't come out here to be farmers but to conquer and take gold, and as for food we would make do along the way.

We pressed on, and on the third day we came to an Indian village whose inhabitants immediately laid hold of their weapons, and as we drew nearer scattered at the sound of our guns, leaving behind some dead. Without an Indian guide who knew the territory, we went ahead and entered the town, and as we were leaving the fieldmaster Bartolomé de Alba, who was worn out from the siege, took off his helmet to mop his brow, and a devil of a boy about twelve years old fired an arrow at him from where he was perched in a tree beside the road, where it led out of the encampment. The arrow lodged in the fieldmaster's eye and he went right over, so badly wounded that he died three days later. We carved the boy into ten thousand pieces.

Meanwhile, the Indians had returned to the village more than ten thousand strong. We fell at them again with such spirit, and butchered so many of them, that blood ran like a river across the plaza, and we chased them to the Dorado River, and beyond, slaughtering all the way.

At this point, the governor ordered us to draw back, which we did, but with little relish for it, seeing how the men had found more than sixty thousand *pesos'* worth of gold dust in the huts of the village, and an infinity more of it along the banks of the river, and they filled their helmets with it. Later, we learned that when the river fell there was gold for the taking, three inches deep, along the banks—on account of which, many of the men begged the governor's leave to subdue the region, but for reasons of his own, he said no.

And that is why many of us, including myself, deserted in the night, and when we had come to a Christian town, went each of us our separate ways. I headed for Centiago and from there to Las Charcas province, my small store of coins dwindling little by little until, before long, I had lost it all.

CHAPTER 10

She goes to the city of La Plata.

I *moved on to La Plata* and found work with Captain Francisco de Aganumen, a rich Basque mine owner. I was with him for a few days, until some unpleasantness broke out between me and another Basquero, one of my new master's friends. While trying to get set up again, I put up in the house of a widow, doña Catalina de Chaves, who was, from what people said, the highest born, most important lady in those parts. I'd struck up a friendship with one of her servants, and it was thanks to him she promised to take me in for a while.

It fell out that, on Holy Thursday, while this lady was going through the stations of the Cross, she collided with doña Francisca Marmolejo, the wife of don Pedro de Andrade, who was the count of Lemos's nephew, and they had some words about who should have first pew in the church. In the end, doña Francisca let doña Catalina have it with one of her clogs, at which point there was a great uproar and people began crowding around.

Doña Catalina went back to her house, followed by a flock of friends and relatives, and there the matter was hotly debated. The other lady remained in the church with a flock of her own backers, not daring to leave until nightfall, when her husband don Pedro arrived with the usual crowd of ministers and deputies, along with the sheriff, don Rafael Ortiz of Soto-mayor, a knight of Malta and now the sheriff of Madrid—all trooping in with their torches lighted to escort her home.

As they made their way down the street that runs from San Francisco to the main square, the noise of swords broke out, and the sheriff, along with the ministers and deputies, headed off, leaving the lady and her husband standing there in the street. At this instant, an Indian ran by, going in the direction of the noise, and as he passed the lady doña Francisca Marmolejo he slashed her face from side to side with a knife or a razor, and kept on running—all of which happened so quickly that the husband, don Pedro, didn't notice at first. But once he realized what had happened, there was a colossal uproar—confusion, noise, the gaggle of onlookers, again the sound of swordplay, prisoners taken—and really, no one had the slightest idea what was going on.

In the meantime the Indian had gone to doña Catalina's house, and as he came in he said to her ladyship, "The deed is done." The mayhem continued, with everyone expecting the worst to happen at any moment—something had to come out of the investigation, and so three days later, the sheriff entered the house of doña Catalina and found her seated in the front parlor.

He made the woman take a solemn oath, and then he asked her if she knew who had cut doña Francisca Marmolejo's face, and she responded, "Si!" He asked her who—and she answered, "A razor, and this hand." And with that the sheriff left, placing some guards around the house.

The questioning of the household began, and when the sheriff got to this one Indian, he scared the pants off him with his threats of the rack, and the lying coward swore up and down that he'd seen me leave the house dressed in Indian clothes and wearing a wig, all of which his mistress had given me, and that it was a Basque barber Francisco Ciguren who had furnished the razor, and that he'd seen me return and heard me say, "The deed is done."

The sheriff arrested the barber and myself, loading us up with chains and keeping us far apart from each other, and from everyone else, too. This went on for a few days, until one night a justice of the high court who had taken up the case and arrested some of the town officials—why, I have no idea— came to the jail and tortured the barber, and before long the barber admitted that he and one other person were guilty. Then the justice came for my confession. I told him I didn't know the first thing about it—he ordered me to be stripped and tied to the rack. A lawyer stuck his head in and pointed out that I was a Basquero, and therefore exempt from torture by the privilege of nobility. The justice didn't pay him any mind, and went on with the proceedings. They gave the screws a turn and I held fast, steady as an oak.

The questions were still coming and the screws still turning when a note arrived, from doña Catalina de Chaves as I later learned, and the justice opened it and read it and then just stood there a while, looking at me. At last he said, "Take the lad down." They got me off the rack and back to my cell, and the justice went home to his house.

The whole thing dragged on somehow, and in the end I was sentenced to ten years in Chile without pay. The barber got two hundred lashes and six years in the galleys. We appealed through our fellow Basqueros, and again the matter dragged on somehow, until one day a ruling came down from the Royal Court saying that I was free to go, that the barber was also free to go, and that doña Francisca was responsible for the court costs.

It just goes to show that persistence and hard work can perform miracles, and it happens regularly—especially in the Indies!

CHAPTER 11

She goes to Charcas.

With *this scrape behind me*, I had no choice but to leave La Plata, and I headed for Charcas some sixteen leagues off. There I met up again with Juan López de Arguijo, the alderman—and he gave me another ten thousand head of llama to drive and a hundred-some-odd Indians. He also gave me a great deal of money to buy wheat in the Cochabamba plains. My job was to grind it and get it to Potosí, where the scarcity of wheat made for high prices. I went and bought eight thousand bushels at four *pesos* a bushel, hauled them by llama to the mills at Guilcomayo, had thirty-five hundred ground into flour and took them to Potosí. I then sold them all at fifteen and a half *pesos* a bushel, went back to the mills, where some of the rest had already been ground, found buyers for it at ten *pesos* a bushel, and brought the cash back to my master in Charcas, who liked the deal so well he sent me back to Cochabamba on the same errand.

One Sunday during this time, in Charcas, when I had nothing better to do, I went to play cards at the house of don Antonio Calderón, the bishop's nephew. The company included the vicar-general, the archdeacon, and a Sevillean merchant who lived with his wife there in town. I sat down to play with the merchant, and the game was going along smoothly until, on one particular hand, the merchant, who was already smarting from his losses, said, "I raise you."

I said, "How much do you raise?" and he said again, "I raise you."

Again I asked, "How much?"

He slammed down a doubloon and said, "I raise you a cuckold's horn!"

"Fine," I said, "I'll see you that horn and raise you the one that's still on your head!"

He swept the cards from the table and drew his dagger. I drew my own, the others at the table grabbed us and pulled us apart, and then we went on playing, with everyone sidestepping the issue, well into the night. I left for home, but hadn't gone far when I turned a corner and who should I meet up with but this same merchant, who draws his sword and comes at me. I pulled out my own blade and we fell to fighting—we parried, but before long I ran him through, and down he went.

The fracas raised a crowd of people, including the police, and they tried to arrest me. I fought them back, taking two wounds in the process, and retreated to the safety of the cathedral. Here I held up for a few days on my master's advice, until, one evening, when the hour seemed ripe, the byways clear, I slipped off to Piscobamba.

CHAPTER 12

She leaves Charcas for Piscobamba.

In *Piscobamba*, I put up for a few days at the house of a friend, Juan Torrico de Zaragoza. One night during supper a card game was mustered with some friends who had dropped by. I paired off with a Portuguese fellow, Fernando de Acosta, a high roller who led off by betting fourteen *pesos* a point. I in turn threw down sixteen points against him, and when he saw my cards he slapped his face and said, "Why, if it isn't the devil himself!"

"How much," I asked him, "have you lost up until now, on the way to becoming such a fool?"

He stretched his hands out, one on either side of my head, and said, "I've lost my father's horns."

With that, I threw my cards down and drew my sword. The Portuguese drew his, and the other players grabbed hold of us and kept us apart, and with their jokes and quips about the hazards of the game they managed to calm us down. Fernando de Acosta paid up and left, apparently in good humor.

Three nights later, about eleven o'clock, I was on my way home when I spotted a man loitering at the corner up ahead. I flipped my cape over my shoulder, pulled my sword from its sheath, and continued toward him. As I came near, he hurled himself on me, jabbing and shouting, "You horned rogue!" I recognized him by his voice and we went at it, I ran him through, and down he went, dead. For a moment, I stood there thinking what to do—I looked around and didn't spot anyone who might have seen us fighting. So I went on to my friend Zaragoza's house, kept my mouth shut, and went to bed.

The next morning, good and early, the sheriff don Pedro de Meneses came and woke me up and took me off with him. As soon as I was in the jailhouse they threw me in leg irons, and about an hour later the sheriff came back with a court clerk to take my statement. I told them I didn't know anything about it—they tried to torture me into talking, but I denied everything. Then they indicted me, evidence came in, I gave my story, and when the case came to trial I found myself face to face with witnesses I'd never laid eyes on before. They sentenced me to death—I appealed, and they ordered that the execution be carried out anyway. Now I was getting worried.

A priest arrived to confess me, and I refused—he insisted, and I held my ground. After this, it rained priests, I was drowning in them—me, a self-professed Lutheran! They dressed me up in a taffeta frock and put me on a horse. The priests cried and pleaded but the sheriff had a mind to hang me, and he told them if I wanted to go to hell, that was my business, he didn't give a damn. They rode me out of the jail and down a series of unfamiliar back streets, all the while trying to keep clear of the priests—and I arrived at the gallows, half out of my mind with the priests' shrieking and flailing, and they started pushing me up the four, rough stairs. The one who was really driving me crazy was a Dominican, brother Andres de San Pablo (I had a nice chat with him, about a year ago, at the college of Atocha in Madrid). I had to stand on tiptoe while they gave me the *volatín*, which is the thin rope they hang you with, but the executioner was still having trouble getting it around my neck, so I said to him, "You drunk! Put it on right, or don't put it on at all—I've got my hands full with these priests!"

In the middle of all of this a messenger rode up from La Plata, dispatched by the secretary under orders from the president, don Diego de Portugal, and at the urging of Martín de Mendiola—a Basquero who had heard about the squeeze I was in. With the town clerk looking on, he handed the sheriff a court order postponing the execution and shifting both prisoner and trial to the Royal Court, some twelve leagues away. Now, the story behind this is a strange one, and it demonstrates the mercy of Almighty God. It seems that the fellows who had testified against me as eyewitnesses in the murder of the Portuguese had run afoul of the law in La Plata—for I don't know what crimes—and they were sentenced to the rope, and when they were at the foot of the gallows, with no inkling of the fix I was in, they admitted they had been bribed to testify against some unknown person in the Piscobamba murder—and so the court got busy, spurred on by Martín de Mendiola, and came up with a stay of execution.

It arrived not a moment too soon, which was wildly to the satisfaction of the sympathetic townsfolk. The sheriff had me taken down from the gallows and sent back to jail, and from there he had me sent under guard to La Plata. I was retried and, thanks to those poor devils who were about to be hanged, acquitted. Their evidence against me was now worthless, and nobody else came forward with anything, and so twenty-four days later they let me go, and I stayed around for a few days after that.

CHAPTER 13

She goes to Cochabamba and returns to La Plata.

From *La Plata*, I headed for the city of Cochabamba to settle some business between my master, Juan López de Arguijo, and one Pedro de Chavarría, a Navarre native living in Cochabamba with his wife, doña María Dávalos, the daughter of the late Captain Juan Dávalos and doña María de Ulloa, who had taken the veil, and was now living in La Plata in a convent she had founded. We settled the accounts, which showed a balance of something like a thousand *pesos* in favor of my master Arguijo. Chavarría handed over the money in a cheerful, businesslike manner, asked me to his house for dinner, and put me up for a few days. I paid my respects and left, after promising Chavarría's wife to visit her mother, the La Plata nun, and deliver messages on her behalf.

Some trifling business with friends kept me in town until the early afternoon. Finally I got started, and my way out took me once again by Chavarría's place. There in the entryway I saw a crowd of people, and I heard squabbling coming from inside. I stopped to see what the story was, and at this very moment doña María Dávalos stuck her head out of the window and cried, "Take me with you, Señor Capitán—my husband is trying to kill me!" And with this, she jumped out the window.

Two friars hurried up at this point and said to me, "You better take her with you. Her husband caught her with don Antonio Calderón, the bishop's nephew, and he killed him— now he has doña María locked up, and has a mind to kill her too." And with that, they hoisted her up on the mule's behind, and off we went.

I didn't stop until eleven that night when I reached the La Plata River. Along the way I passed one of Chavarría's servants coming from La Plata. I tried to keep my distance, hiding our faces beneath my cloak, but as it turned out he must have recognized us and gone on ahead and told his master.

The sight of that river set me shaking—the water was high and I couldn't tell how we were going to get across.

"Let's go," the señora said, "we have no choice, God help us!"

I dismounted and looked around for a place to cross. Determined to brave it, I climbed back up and with my lady in distress on the mule's behind I plunged into the water, and kept on going, until, with the help of God, we came to the other side. I rode up to an inn just a little ways further on and woke up the innkeeper, who was startled to see someone at that late hour and to find we had crossed the river. I foddered my mule and gave it a rest, the innkeeper gave us some eggs and bread and fruit, we wrung out our clothes as best we could and saddled up again and set off, and there in the first light at dawn, some five leagues down the road, we saw the city of La Plata in the distance.

We continued toward La Plata, somewhat cheered by the sight, but suddenly doña María tightened her arms around me and cried, "Oh, señor—my husband!"

I turned, and there he was, coming up behind us on a horse that looked half-dead from the road. His being there was a wonder all right—I'd left Cochabamba way ahead of him, while he was still in his house, and made straight for the river without stopping once, crossed it, put up at the inn for an hour at best, and then set out again—and that wasn't the half of it. The servant I met in the road must have warned him—but still, he needed time to get back to Cochabamba, and Chavarría himself needed time to saddle up and leave. So what was he doing here? I couldn't figure it out—unless, in my ignorance of the roads, I had taken a more roundabout way.

Anyway, there he was about thirty yards off, and he took a shot at us with a rifle and missed, the bullet whizzing by so close to our ears we could hear it sing. I spurred my mule on and plunged down a brambly hill and didn't see Chavarría again, which makes me think his horse must have given out.

After four long leagues, going breakneck the whole way, I got to La Plata in a pitiful state, knocked at the door of the Augustine convent, and handed doña María Dávalos over to her mother. As I turned to get back on my mule, I collided with Pedro de Chavarría, who came at me sword in hand without bothering to wait for an explanation.

He gave me a turn, appearing like that out of nowhere, with me bone tired and him, the poor man, still thinking I had done him wrong. Still, I drew my weapon and took my stand. We clashed swords all the way into the church, and he must have been good, because he poked me twice in the breast before I could get in a single hit. That woke me up, and I went at him, backing him up against the altar. He took a huge swipe at my head, I fended it off with my dagger and drove my blade a span's length between his ribs.

By now, such a crowd had gathered we couldn't go on. The police showed up and tried to drag us out of the church, and with that two Franciscans from across the way slipped me into their monastery, under the conniving eye of the constable don

Pedro Beltrán, my master Juan López de Arguijo's brother in-law. The friars kindly took me in and looked to my wounds, and I held up in the monastery, convalescing, for five months.

Chavarría was also a long time mending—all the while clamoring for them to hand over his wife. Statements were taken, efforts were made, and she resisted, claiming her life was plainly in danger. Finally the bishop and the president and some other dignitaries got into it and arranged for them both to take holy vows—she right where she was, and he wherever he liked.

Still, there was the matter of my own case. My master Juan López de Arguijo came forward and told the archibishop, don Alonso de Peralta, and the president and the other dignitaries how I had become involved in the affair, innocently, altogether by chance, and without malice, despite what the other gentleman said, and how I had no choice but to help the woman in question, who had thrown herself at me fleeing bloody murder, and how I had delivered her up to her mother as she had begged me to do. When all of this was attested to and confirmed, they were satisfied, the case ended, and Pedro de Chavarría and his wife went off to their monasteries.

I came out of hiding, settled my affairs, and went quite often to visit my little nun and her mother, and some of the other ladies there, all of whom were invariably pleased by my company and made me many gifts of this, that, and the other thing.

CHAPTER 14

She travels from La Plata to Piscobamba, and from there to Mizque.

I *needed to make* a living somehow. The lady doña María de Ulloa, who was grateful for my services, persuaded the president and the Court to send me on commission to Piscobamba and the plains of Mizque, to investigate and punish certain crimes that had been reported in the area. They set me up with a court clerk and a constable, and we set off together.

When I came to Piscobamba, I indicted and arrested a certain Lieutenant Francisco de Escobar, who lived there with his wife, on charges that he had robbed two Indians, murdered them in a most cowardly fashion, and buried them under his house, which was situated in a quarry. We dug around and found the bodies. I tracked down every last detail of the case, and when I was through I called the parties before me and sentenced the defendant to death. He appealed, I granted him his appeal, and the case shifted to the Court in La Plata along with the accused. But in La Plata, the sentence was upheld and Escobar was hanged. I headed on to the plains of Mizque and took care of my business there and, reporting back to La Plata, I handed over the Mizque documents and stayed on for a few days.

CHAPTER 15

She travels to La Paz and murders a man.

I *moved on to La Paz*, where I rested for a little while without event, until one day, without a care in the world, I stopped by the sheriff don Antonio Barraza's to chat with one of his servants. And I tell you, the devil must have been stirring the coals, because it ended with the fellow calling me a liar and slapping me across the face with his cap. I unsheathed my dagger and down he went. A crowd of people pounced on me all at once, so that I was wounded, arrested, hauled off to jail, and they tended my wounds at the same time they tried me for murder. When the charges were upheld, along with a heap of others, the sheriff sentenced me to death. I appealed, but the man ordered me to be hanged anyway.

I spent two full days confessing. On the third, mass was held in the jail, and when the priest had taken communion he gave it to me and turned back to the altar, and I instantly spat the wafer out into my right hand, shouting madly, "I CALL ON THE CHURCH! I CALL ON THE CHURCH!"

Complete bedlam ensued. The brothers were scandalized and kept shouting, "Heretic! Heretic!" and at the sound of the uproar the priest turned around and told everyone to keep clear of me. Then he finished the mass, and at this point the head bishop, a Dominican brother, Domingo de Valderrama, walked in along with the governor. The priests circled round me, along with a great number of townspeople   they lighted candles, unfurled a canopy over my head and carried me in procession into the sacristy, where everyone got down on their knees and a priest pried the wafer from my hand and placed it in the tabernacle—exactly where I don't know, because I didn't see. They scraped at my hand, washing it again and again, and dried it off—then everyone disappeared, leaving me there alone. This was a scheme I had come up with thanks to a pious Franciscan, who gave me some words of wisdom when I was in jail, and took my last confession.

The governor kept the church surrounded, with me under lock and key, for a month or so, and then the guard was removed. One of the local priests reconnoitered the roads and outlying hills, gave me a mule and a little cash—on orders from the head bishop, I can only guess—and I slipped away down the road to Cuzco.

CHAPTER 16

She leaves for the city of Cuzco.

I *came to Cuzco*, a city just as grand as Lima in both riches and people. As the bishop's seat, it boasts a cathedral dedicated to the Ascension of Our Lady, which is served by five prebendaries, eight canons, eight parishes, and four monasteries (of Franciscans, Dominicans, Augustines, and Mercedarians), along with four schools, two nunneries, and three hospitals.

I'd only been there a few days when I got myself into another serious mess, undeserved to tell the truth, because this time around I was entirely blameless—whatever you may have heard. What happened was that one night out of the blue a man was murdered, one don Luis de Godoy, who was the sheriff of Cuzco, a talented caballero and the highest-born man in those parts. Later, it came out he was murdered by a fellow named Carranza over a list of grievances too long to go into, but no one knew this at the time and they lit upon me instead. The sheriff Fernando de Guzmán had me arrested and for five months he kept me miserable and uncomfortable, until Almighty God saw to it that the truth came out, and along with it my total innocence in the matter—and with that, they let me go, and I cleared out of Cuzco.

CHAPTER 17

She moves on to Lima, joins the sea battle
against the Dutch, is cast overboard, and is
rescued by the Dutch fleet, which leaves her on
the coast of Paita, whence she returns to Lima.

I *arrived in Lima* in the days when don Juan de Mendoza
y Luna, the marquis of Montes Claros, was the viceroy of
Peru.

The Dutch were laying siege to Lima with eight warships
that had been stationed off the coast, and the city was armed
to the teeth. We went out to meet them from the port of
Callao in five ships, and for a long time it went well for us, but
then the Dutch began hammering away at our flagship and in
the end she heaved over and only three of us managed to
escape—me, a barefoot Franciscan friar, and a soldier—pad-
dling around until an enemy ship took us up. The Dutch
treated us like dirt, jeering and scoffing. All the others who
had been on the flagship had drowned. Four ships remained
under General don Rodrigo de Mendoza, and when they got
back to Callao the next morning at least nine hundred men
were reckoned as missing, myself included, because I'd been
on the flagship.

For twenty-six days I was in enemy hands, thinking they
meant to deal with me by carting me off to Holland. But in the
end they flung me and my two companions out on the Paita

coast, a good hundred leagues from Lima, and after several days and no end of trouble a good man took pity on our naked state, gave us some clothes and gear and pointed us in the direction of Lima, and we finally made it back.

I stayed in Lima some seven months, getting by as best I could. I bought a cheap horse that suited me fine and I made the rounds on it for a couple of days, all the while turning over and over in my head whether I should head back to Cuzco. One day, when I'd just about made up my mind, I was passing through the plaza when a constable approached and told me that the mayor, don Juan de Espinosa, a knight of Santiago, wanted to see me. When I got to his honor's house there were two soldiers waiting there, and no sooner had I entered than one of them said, "This is the one, señor. This is the missing horse, and we can prove it."

The deputies surrounded me and the mayor said, "Well, what do we have here?" The whole thing was so sudden that I didn't know what to say, and there I stood, confounded and stammering, the very picture of guilt, when it suddenly occurred to me to take off my cloak and throw it over the horse's head.

"Señor," I said, "I implore your honor, ask these gentlemen which is the eye this horse is blind in—the right or the left. It's entirely possible that this is another animal, and these gentlemen are mistaken."

"Good idea," the mayor said. "You two, answer together, which eye is this horse blind in?" The two of them were confused now, and the mayor repeated, "Together now, at the same time."

"In the left eye," one said, and the other said, "In the right—the left, I mean!" and the mayor said, "A fine story, you can't even get it straight!" and they came back at him, the two of them in unison now, "No, it's the left, the left, we both say so—no mistaking it."

I said, "Señor, this is no proof. One says one thing and the other says something else."

"No, we both agree," one of them said, "the horse is blind in its left eye. I was going to say left, but I accidentally made a mistake—but then I corrected myself. It's the left, I tell you."

The mayor paused for a moment and I asked, "Señor, what is your honor's decision?"

He replied, "I say that if this is all the proof they have, adiós, you can go on your way."

With that, I swept off the cloak. "Look, your honor," I said, "they're both lying. This horse isn't blind at all!" The mayor got up and came over to the horse, and looked at it, and said, "Take your horse, vaya con Dios," and then he turned to the others and had them arrested.

I saddled up and left at that point and I never learned how it ended, because I was already on my way to Cuzco.

CHAPTER 18

In Cuzco, she kills the New Cid
and is herself wounded.

And so once again I found myself in Cuzco. I put up at the treasurer Lope de Alcedo's house and stayed there for some time. One day, I went to a friend's house to gamble, the two of us sat down to a friendly game of cards, and everything was going along fine until a dark, hairy giant of a man sat down next to me, a menacing fellow everyone called The Cid. I went on with my game and won the hand I was playing, but then The Cid stuck his paw in my winnings, palmed some of my gold, and walked out.

Before long he was back, helping himself to another fistful and loitering around behind my back. I slipped out my dagger and went on with the game, and the next time he stuck his paw out I saw it coming, and skewered his hand to the table with my blade. I jumped up and drew my sword, the others took out theirs, and then The Cid's partners joined in and got me so penned up I took three hits—I slipped out into the street, which was a piece of luck, seeing as how they were about to chop me into pieces.

The Cid was the first to come after me. I took a swipe at him, only to discover he was trussed up in armor like a brass watch. The others tumbled out and fell upon me. Just in that instant, two Basqueros happened to be walking by, and when

they heard the commotion they stopped, and seeing as how I
was one against five they took up alongside of me—and still,
the three of us got the worst of it, with The Cid and his men
backing us all the way down the street to where it opened into
the square. And as we drew near the church of San Francisco,
The Cid gave me such a stab from behind with his dagger that
the blade ran clean through my left shoulder—and one of the
others plunged his sword a hand's width into my left side, and
I fell to the ground in a sea of my own blood.

With that, everyone turned tail and ran. I pulled myself to
my feet, the taste of death in my mouth, and saw The Cid
standing by the church door. I staggered toward him and he
came at me, saying, "You dog—still alive?" and thrust at me
with his blade. I forced the blow off to the side with my dagger, and with a bit of luck managed to find the unprotected
soft of his belly with my blade, pushed it clear through him,
and he fell to the ground, begging for a priest. I went down as
well, and the ruckus brought a flock of people, including two
friars and the sheriff don Pedro de Córdoba, a knight of Santiago. When he saw his deputies preparing to arrest me, he
said, "What are you thinking? All that remains to be done is
their last confessions."

The Cid died right there on the spot. Some goodhearted
people took me to the treasurer's house, where I was staying,
and they put me to bed, but they wouldn't allow the surgeon
to start in on me until I had made my confession—they were
so scared I was going to die right there, from one moment to
the next. Brother Luis Ferrer de Valencia, who is a great man,
arrived and took my confession—and seeing as how I was
about to die, I told him the truth about myself. He was aston-
ished, and he absolved me of my sins, and encouraged me to
take heart and tried to comfort me. Then they brought me the

last sacrament and I took it, and from that moment on I seemed to feel my strength returning.

The surgery began and I felt every cut, and what with the pain and loss of blood I finally passed out. I was unconscious for fourteen hours, and the whole time that saint, brother Luis Ferrer, never left my side—may God reward him! I came to crying out for Saint Joseph—and the whole way through I had some divine assistance, which God will grant us in our hour of greatest need. The third day arrived, and then the fifth, at which point I allowed myself to hope a little.

Out of fear of the law they moved me one night to the Franciscan monastery, and put me in the cell of brother Martín de Aróstegui, one of my friend Alcedo's kinsmen, and I stayed there for four months, convalescing. When the sheriff heard of my whereabouts, he blustered about and put guards in the neighborhood and blocked all the roads. By this time, I was on the mend and could see that my days in Cuzco were numbered, and I also figured the dead man's friends were bent on killing me, and taking all of this into account, with the help and advice of some friends of my own, I decided on a change of scene.

Captain **Gaspar de Carranza** gave me a thousand *pesos*, Lope de Alcedo, the treasurer, I mentioned earlier, gave me three mules and some weapons, and don Francisco de Arzaga gave me three slaves—and so, in the company of two trusty Basqueros, I left Cuzco one night, headed for Guamanga.

CHAPTER 19

She leaves Cuzco for Guamanga,
crossing the bridge near Andahuailas,
and passing through Guancavélica.

I *left Cuzco*, as I said, and had gotten as far as the Apurí-
mac Bridge when I ran into the law, along with some friends
of The Cid, all waiting there for me. "You're under arrest,"
the constable said, and tried to take me into custody with the
help of eight other fellows. The five of us spread out and the
fighting began, sometimes squaring off one man against another, sometimes in groups. One of my black slaves went
down almost immediately, I heard one of theirs cry out in
pain, and then another—and then my other slave went down.
I leveled the constable with a shot from my pistol, and when
his troop heard the sound of gunfire they took off, leaving
three of theirs stretched out on the ground.

Now, the jurisdiction of Cuzco goes up to the bridge I've
just mentioned, and no further, so that my comrades accompanied me to that point and then turned back, leaving me to
continue on my way alone. I continued on to Andahuailas,
and when I got there I immediately bumped into the sheriff,
who was very friendly, all manners, and even offered to put
me up in his house and asked me to join him for supper, but I
declined his hospitality, thinking perhaps the man was a little
too courteous—and off I went.

I made it to the city of Guancavélica, pulled up at an inn, and remained there a couple of days, scouting the place out. And one day, when I was in the little square just at the foot of Mercury Hill, I spotted Doctor Solarzano, the justice of the court of Lima, who was there as an official guest of the governor, don Pedro Osario. I saw a constable approach him (this constable, I later discovered, goes by the name of Pedro Xuárez), and the judge turned his head and looked at me, then took out a piece of paper, looked at it, looked back at me, and I saw the constable and a Negro start quickly in my direction.

I strolled on as if I didn't have a care in the world, while in truth my cares were piling up like flies on meat—a couple more steps, and suddenly there's the constable, standing in front of me, and he pulls my hat from my head, I pull his hat off, and the Negro comes up from behind and tries to twist me up in my cloak. So I slip out of the cloak, draw my sword with one hand and my pistol with the other, and the two of them come at me with their swords. I unload my pistol and the constable goes down—I lunge at the Negro and before long he falls with a knife wound. I take off running and come across an Indian leading a horse down the road (I found out later the horse belonged to the mayor), I relieve him of it, jump into the saddle and ride off for Guamanga, some fourteen leagues off.

Once I had the Balsas River behind me, I stopped to rest my horse, and as I stood there what should I see but three men on horseback gallop up to the river and then wade halfway across. My heart was in my mouth and I could barely say the words, "Caballeros, what brings you here?"

One of them answered, "Your own arrest, Señor."

I drew my weapons, loaded two pistols, and replied, "If you've gotten it in your heads to take me alive . . . that cannot he First, you will have to kill me, and then you can arrest me," and I moved closer to the riverbank.

"Capitán," one of the others said, "we're under orders, and we had to come. The truth is we would like nothing better than to serve you, Señor, not kill you"—and all of this with the three of them standing there in the middle of the river.

I told them their kind words were much appreciated, placed three doubloons on a nearby stone, mounted up and, after paying them my respects, took off again on the road to Guamanga.

CHAPTER 20

Her entrance into Guamanga, and what
happens to her there up until she reveals
herself to the senior bishop.

I *entered the city* of Guamanga and went to an inn. There I met a soldier who was just passing through, and he took a fancy to the horse, which I sold him for two hundred *pesos*. I then went out to see the city, and it struck me as a fine one, full of beautiful buildings—the most handsome I'd seen in all of Peru.

I counted three monasteries (of Franciscans, Dominicans, and Mercedarians), a nunnery, and a hospital. There are a great many Indians living there, and many Spaniards, too—and the soil is good, because the city is situated on a great plain that is neither too cold nor too warm, and there are fields upon fields of wheat, and grapes for wine-making, and other fruits and grains. The cathedral is a grand one, with three prebendaries, two canons, and a good bishop, the Augustine friar don Agustín de Carvajal, who was of great service to me until his sudden death in the year 1620—they say he had served as bishop there since the year 1612.

I was in town for several days, and my miserable luck saw to it that I ended up on a number of occasions in a local gambling house, and on one such occasion the sheriff don Baltasar de Quiñones came in, looked me over and, not recognizing me, asked where I was from. I told him I came from the Basque country.

"And where do you come from now?" he asked.

"From Cuzco," I replied.

He paused a moment, looking at me, and said, "You're under arrest."

I replied, "It will be my pleasure," and drew my sword as I backed toward the door.

The sheriff cried out for help in the name of the king, and I met with such resistance when I came to the doorway that I couldn't get through. Pulling out a three-barreled pistol, I managed to get out, and disappeared into the house of an acquaintance I had made there. The sheriff went off and proceeded to confiscate my mule and the few small possessions I had with me at the inn.

When I learned that my new acquaintance was a Basquero, I put up at his house for a number of days. And all the while, there was no word of the case, no sign that the law was pursuing the matter, but still, it seemed like a good idea for me to move on—after all, why should the law be any different here than in some other town? And so, determined to slip away the first chance I got, I set off one afternoon just as night was falling, and I hadn't gone more than a few steps when, as my miserable luck would have it, I came face to face with two constables.

"Who goes there?" they ask me.

"Friends," I say.

And then they ask for my name and I say (what I shouldn't have said), "The devil," and the two of them step up, trying to grab me, and I draw my sword, and this causes a great commotion.

"In the name of the law!" they begin to shout, and people

come running. The sheriff had been in the bishop's house, and now he steps out into the street— other officers circle around me, I can see I'm in a real fix now, and I fire one of my pistols and someone goes down. The situation is becoming more and more desperate with every second, and I turn to discover the Basque friend at my side and some other Basqueros along with him. The sheriff has been shouting for someone to kill me—and shots ring out on both sides.

At this point, the bishop stepped out of his palace with four torchbearers at his side, and walked right into the middle of the whole thing, guided in my direction by his secretary, Juan Bautista de Arteaga. He reached me and said, "Señor Lieutenant, give me your weapons."

I told him, "Señor, there are a great many men who would like nothing better than to catch me without them."

"Give them to me," he said. "You are safe with me, and I give you my word I will take you from here unharmed—even if it should cost me my life."

"Esteemed señor," I said, "when we are safely in the church, I will kiss Your Holiness's feet." And then four of the sheriff's slaves come at me, pushing me back—and they attacked so ferociously, and with so little regard for the bishop's presence, that I was forced to get into the hand and knock one of them clear off his feet. The bishop's secretary put himself at my side with his sword and shield, while the other men in his retinue cried out, condemning the disrespect to His Eminence, and with that the struggle eased a little. His Holiness held me fast by the arm, relieved me of my weapons and, placing himself at my side, he took me with him into his house.

He immediately saw to it that a small wound I had taken was dressed and ordered that I be given supper and a place to rest, and then he locked me in the room and took the key with him. Soon afterward the sheriff arrived, and His Holiness had a long discussion with the man, and they argued bitterly over the whole matter, as I later learned.

The next morning at about ten o'clock, His Eminence had me brought before him and asked me who I was, where I was from, who my parents were, and the whole course of my life—the various events and byroads that had brought me there. I gave it to him piecemeal, mixing in bits of good advice and wise words as to the hazards of life, the terrors of death, the various contingencies that might bring one to that unfortunate state—and the fear a man has of passing on to the next world without having prepared himself—and all the while I was speaking, I felt a calm sweeping over me, I felt as if I were humbled before God, that things were simpler than they had seemed before, and that I was very small and insignificant. And seeing that he was such a saintly man, and feeling as if I might already be in the presence of God, I revealed myself to the bishop and told him, "Señor, all of this that I have told you . . . in truth, it is not so. The truth is this: that I am a woman, that I was born in such and such a place, the daughter of this man and this woman, that at a certain age I was placed in a certain convent with a certain aunt, that I was raised there and took the veil and became a novice, and that when I was about to profess my final vows, I left the convent for such and such a reason, went to such and such a place, undressed myself and dressed myself up again, cut my hair, traveled here and there, embarked, disembarked, hustled, killed, maimed, wreaked havoc, and roamed about, until coming to a stop in this very instant, at the feet of Your Eminence."

My tale lasted until one in the morning, and all the while that saintly gentleman sat there motionless, without speaking or even batting an eyelid, listening to my story, and when I had finished he didn't say a word but remained there motionless, his face bright with tears. Afterward, he sent me to rest and eat. Then he rang for the chaplain and had me brought to an old chapel, where I was given a table and a mattress—then they locked the door behind me and I lay down and fell asleep.

That afternoon around four, the bishop called for me again and spoke to me with a great kindness, urging me to thank God for His mercy in showing me that I had been traveling the road of the lost, the road that leads straight to eternal punishment. He told me to think about my life and to make a true confession, which shouldn't be too hard, since I had already confessed, more or less—and afterward, God would help us to see what must be done. With this, and other such wisdom, the afternoon drew to a close. I returned to my room, was given a good meal, and went to bed.

The next morning the bishop said mass, which I heard, and then gave thanks. He invited me to have breakfast with him, and continued his lecture, letting me know in the end that mine was the most astonishing case of its kind he had heard in all his life.

"So . . . ," he concluded, "is it true?"

"Yes, señor," I answered.

"I'm sure you will understand if I tell you that your strange tale raises some doubts."

"Señor—" I said, "it is the truth, and if it will remove your doubts, let other women examine me—I will submit to such a test."

"I am glad to hear you say this," he replied. "I will arrange it."

I then left, as it was his hour to receive visitors. At midday I ate and rested a little, and toward four in the afternoon two old women came in and looked me over and satisfied them selves, declaring afterward before the bishop that they had examined me and found me to be a woman, and were ready to swear to it under oath, if necessary and that what's more they had found me to be an intact virgin, as on the day I came into the world. This piece of news touched His Eminence. He dismissed the women and sent for me, along with the chaplain, and in his presence he lovingly embraced me.

"Daughter," he said, "my doubt is gone. I believe you now, and I shall believe from this day on whatever you may choose to tell me—I esteem you as one of the more remarkable people in this world, and promise to help you in whatever you do, and to aid you in your new life in service to God."

He ordered that I be placed in decent quarters, and there in comfort I prepared my confession, which I made to the best of my ability, and afterward His Eminence gave me communion. It seems that word of my case had gotten out, drawing a large crowd of people to the palace, and those of name and position had to be let in, no matter how much it displeased me—or the bishop, for that matter.

Six days later, when all was said and done, His Eminence arranged for my entrance into the nunnery of Santa Clara, which at the time was Guamanga's only order of religious women, and once again I donned the veil. His Eminence left the palace with me at his side, and we made our way slowly through a crowd so huge, it was hard to believe there was anyone left at home, or that we would ever get to the church. Finally, we came around to the convent gate, for it was impossible to enter at the main doors, as His Eminence had planned.

All the nuns were there, bearing lighted candles, and a written promise was given by the abbess and the senior nuns, stating that the convent would release me into the keeping of

His Eminence, or his successor, whenever they should ask for me. The bishop embraced me and gave me his blessing and I went inside. I was carried in procession to the choir, where I said a prayer. I kissed the abbess's hand, embraced and was embraced in turn by each of the nuns, and then made my way to the visiting room, where the bishop was waiting for me. He offered me good counsel, exhorting me to be a good Christian and give thanks to the Lord. He bade me take the sacraments, offering to come as often as I wished him to for this purpose, and indeed, he did so on many occasions.

News of this event had spread far and wide, and it was a source of amazement to the people who had known me before, and to those who had only heard of my exploits in the Indies, and to those who were hearing of them now for the first time.

Within five months from that time, in the year 1620, my saintly bishop had suddenly died, a grave loss to me.

CHAPTER 21

She leaves Guamanga for Lima, at the
archbishop's command, dressed as a nun
and enters a Trinity convent. Leaving there,
she returns to Guamanga and continues on
toward Santa Fe de Bogotá and Tenerife.

Shortly *after* the bishop died, I was sent for by the archbishop of Lima, His Eminence Señor don Bartolomé Lobo
Guerrero, who became archbishop in 1607 and died on the
twelfth of January in 1622. The nuns were beside themselves
when they took their leave of me, and I was carried off in
a litter with a retinue of six priests, four friars, and six
swordsmen.

It was already dark when we entered Lima, but there were
more people waiting than we knew what to do with, all come
out of curiosity, hoping to catch a glimpse of the Lieutenant
Nun. As for me, I was anxious to get inside the archbishop's
palace, and they lowered me down at the gate.

I kissed His Eminence's hand and he welcomed me warmly
and gave me shelter for the night. The next morning I was
taken to the palace of viceroy don Francisco de Borja, count of
Mayalde and prince of Esquilache, who served in Lima from
1615 to 1622. I dined with him that day and returned in the

evening to the archbishop's, where I found a good supper and comfortable quarters.

On the following day, His Eminence told me I should choose the convent in which I would like to remain. I asked leave to visit them all, which he granted, and I looked at every one, staying in each of them for four or five days. Finally, I settled on the convent of The Most Holy Trinity, of the order of Saint Bernard—a grand convent housing one hundred nuns of the black veil, fifty nuns of the white veil, ten novitiates, ten patronesses, and sixteen servants.

I remained there in all for two years and five months, until word arrived from Spain that I wasn't, nor had I ever been, a professed nun, and with that I was assured I might leave, the sisters bade me a sad farewell, and I set out on my way back to Spain.

I left at once for Guamanga to say my good-byes to the ladies of the convent of Santa Clara, and they held me up there for eight days, during which we enjoyed each other's company and exchanged many gifts and finally, when it was time for me to go, many tears.

I continued on my way to Santa Fe de Bogotá in the kingdom of New Granada, and there I saw the archbishop, Julián de Cortázar, who kept prodding me to stay and take up residence in a convent of my order. I told the man that I had no order, and no religion, and that I was simply trying to get back to my country, where I would do from one day to the next whatever it was that my salvation required. And so, with this, and a fine gift Cortázar gave me, I took my leave.

I went on to Zaragoza, by way of the upper waters of the Magdalena River. There I fell sick, and the place struck me as rife with pestilence, no place for a Spaniard, and I became sicker and sicker each day until I was all but knocking at death's door. After convalescing for some while, but still without even the strength to stand on my feet, a doctor persuaded me to leave, and I set off down the river for the city of Tenerife, and I wasn't there but a few short days when already I had recovered completely.

CHAPTER 22

She embarks in Tenerife and sails to Cartagena,
and from there leaves with the fleet for Spain.

In Tenerife, I learned that the armada of General Tomás
de Larraspuru was about to set sail for Spain. I embarked in
the captain's ship in the year 1624, and was well received by
the general, regaled, invited to dine at his table, and things
went on like this for more than two hundred leagues, well
past the Straits of Bahama. But then one day a quarrel arose
over a game of cards, and I was forced to cut another man's
face with a little knife I had on me, and the event caused
a great deal of disquiet. The general found himself obliged to
remove me and planned to transfer me to the flagship, where
there were other Basqueros. I couldn't have been more
pleased, but I asked to be transferred to the tendership, the
San Telmo, whose captain don Andrés de Otón was carrying
military dispatches, and this was granted. But in the end it
was more trouble than it was worth, because the little boat
was taking on water and we were constantly in danger of going under.

Thanks to God, we made it to Cádiz on the first of Novem-
ber, 1624. We disembarked and I remained for eight days,
enjoying the hospitality of Señor don Fadrique de Toledo,
who was general of the armada. As it turned out, two of my

brothers were in his command and I became acquainted with them, and as an honor to me, a great honor, the general took one of them into his personal service and gave the other a promotion.

CHAPTER 23

She departs Cádiz for Seville, and Seville
for Madrid and Pamplona, on her way to Rome,
but having been robbed in the Piedmont,
she returns to Spain.

I *left Cádiz for Seville,* where I spent fifteen days, lying low as much as possible and fleeing from the swarms of people that turned up everywhere, trying to catch a glimpse of me in men's clothing. From there I went on to Madrid, where I managed to go unnoticed for some twenty days. In Madrid, I was arrested on orders from the vicar—I have no idea why—and later set free by Count Olivares. I found work with Count Javier, who was bound for Pamplona, and I went there with him and remained in his service for what must have been about two months.

It was the holy year of the great Jubilee, and so I quit the count's service and left Pamplona for Rome. I set off through France, putting up with a great deal of trouble along the way, for while I was traveling through the Piedmont, in the city of Turin, I was accused of being a Spanish spy and arrested, and they pilfered what little money I had, along with the clothes off my back, and kept me in jail for five days. At the end of that time, I was set free, I can only guess because they had made their investigation and come up with nothing against me— but still, they ordered me to turn back, under penalty of the rope if I refused. So back I went, penniless, barefoot, reduced to begging door to door. In Toulouse, I presented myself before the count of Agramonte, viceroy of Pau and governor of Bayon, to whom I had already delivered letters from Spain. The good man was sorry to see me in such a state, and ordered that I be clothed and fed, and when I left, he gave me one hundred crowns for my journey and a horse—and I went on my way.

I came to Madrid and presented myself before the king, and begged him to reward my many services, which I outlined in a memoir that I placed in the royal hand. The king referred me to the Council on the Indies, and there I went to present what few papers I had managed to snatch from the wreck of my life. They received me and ruled in my favor, granting me, at the king's suggestion, a pension of eight hundred crowns a year, which is a little less than the sum I had asked for. These events occurred in the month of August, in the year 1625. A few other things happened to me while at the Court, but since they don't add up to much, I omit them from these pages.

The king left soon after for the Court of Aragon, arriving in Zaragoza in the early days of January, 1626.

CHAPTER 24

She leaves Madrid for Barcelona.

I *set out for Barcelona* with three companions who were headed for that city. We got as far as Lérida, rested a little, and resumed our journey on Holy Thursday, sometime during the afternoon. As we drew near Velpuche, at what must have been about four in the afternoon, we were ambling along in fine spirits and with little thought of danger, when we rounded a turn and from out of the brush on the left side of the road nine men suddenly sprang at us, with their guns raised and cocked. They circled round us and ordered us to dismount. We had little choice in the matter—truth to tell, we were lucky to get off our horses alive. And so as we stood there, they took our weapons and horses, the clothes we wore and whatever else we had, and left us with nothing more than our papers—which we had to beg for, and which they looked over and handed back—but other than that, they left us with nothing, not even the lint in our pockets.

We continued down the road, embarrassed and naked, entering Barcelona after nightfall on Easter Sunday, 1626, and without the slightest idea, myself at least, what to do. My companions went off this way and that in search of help—I went from house to house crying out that I had been robbed, and in this way I managed to collect a few poor threads, along with a shoddy cloak that I pulled around my shoulders. The night grew darker and I took shelter in a gateway where some other wretches were already stretched out. It was there I learned that the king was in town, attended by the marquis of Montes Claros, a fine gentleman and a philanthropist, with whom I had spoken in Madrid. I went to him the next morning to tell him of the disastrous turn my fortunes had taken—he wept to see me like that, and immediately ordered that I be clothed and, good man that he was, arranged to present me to the king.

I came before His Majesty, and told him the sorry tale of my travels. He listened, and then he asked, "Well, how is it that you allowed yourself to be robbed?"

"Señor," I responded, "I had no choice in the matter."

"How many were there?"

"Nine," I said, "with shotguns, already cocked, and they took us all of a sudden as we were passing through bush country." He indicated with a gesture of his hand that I should approach and hand him my memoir. I kissed his hand, placed my papers in it, and the king said, "I will have a look at it." In the meantime, he had gotten to his feet, and he left the room. I went on my way, and it wasn't long before I was told that the king had granted me four times the allowance of a part-time lieutenant, along with thirty ducats for expenses and the hardship I had suffered.

With that, I said good-bye to the marquis of Montes Claros, to whom I owe so much, and shipped out on the *San Martin*, a Sicilian galley bound for Genoa.

CHAPTER 25

She leaves Barcelona for Genoa, going on from there to Rome.

We set sail from Barcelona and came to Genoa before long, where I remained for fifteen days. During that time, I had an opportunity to pay a visit to Pedro de Chavarría, who was now the inspector general of the Order of Santiago, and one morning I went to his house.

Perhaps it was too early, however, for I was not admitted, and I wandered around for a while killing time. I sat down on a rock by the palace gate where Prince Doria lives, and while I was sitting there a man came up and sat down. He was well dressed in a soldier's uniform, all press and polish, with a fine head of hair, and I recognized him by his speech to be an Italian. We greeted each other and began to talk.

"You, sir, are a Spaniard," he said. I told him yes, I was.

"Most likely then, you are arrogant—that is the way with the Spanish—arrogant and pompous, though I tell you I never saw much there that was worth bragging about."

"I know many," I answered, "who are true men, and quite capable of handling whatever life sends their way."

"I know many as well," he said, "and it's been my experience they are about as handy as a turd."

"Sir, do not say such things," I said, rising to my feet. "It has been my experience that the sorriest Spaniard is many times better than the best Italian."

"Do you have some metal to back up that mouth of yours?" he said.

"But, of course."

"Now's as good a time as any," he said.

"Yes . . . as good a time as any!"

And the two of us stepped behind some water cisterns that were there nearby, and we drew our swords and began to spar, and in that instant I spot another fellow who takes up the Italian's side. Knifeplay—that was their game—swordplay was mine, and I lunged, running the Italian through, and down he went. I still had the other one to finish off, and I was driving him back when a sprightly cripple—his friend, I guess—takes the man's side and begins to drive me back the other direction. Then, a passing acquaintance of mine appeared and, seeing as how I was fighting alone, he took my side. After that, so many joined in that the whole thing was confusion, which was a bit of luck, because that way I was able to clear out without anyone noticing, and make for the galley, and I never did find out what became of all those fellows fighting like that in the street. Once I got on board, I tended to a small wound in my hand. This would have been during the time that the marquis of Santa Cruz was in Genoa.

I left Genoa for Rome. I kissed the feet of the Blessed Pope Urban the Eighth, and told him in brief and as well as I could the story of my life and travels, the fact that I was a woman, and that I had kept my virginity. His Holiness seemed amazed to hear such things, and graciously gave me leave to pursue my life in men's clothing, all the while reminding me it was my duty to lead an honest existence from that day forward, that I must refrain from harming my fellow creatures, and that His

commandment, Thou Shalt Not Kill, carried with it the ven-
geance of God for those who transgressed. My fame had
spread abroad, and it was remarkable to see the throng that
followed me about—famous people, princes, bishops,
cardinals. Indeed, wherever I went, people's doors were
open, and in the six weeks I spent in Rome, scarcely a day
went by when I did not dine with princes. On one Friday, I
was invited by some gentlemen to supper, and they made me
various gifts of this and that, and then, on special orders from
the Roman Senate, wrote my name in a book as an honorary
Roman citizen. On Saint Peter's day, the 29th of June, 1626,
I was taken to the chapel at Saint Peter's, and there I saw all
of the cardinals and attended the ceremonies of the day. All of
them—or most of them—seemed remarkably pleased, even
moved, to share my company, and they spoke to me a great
deal. At one point, during the afternoon, I found myself chat-
ting with three cardinals, one of whom, Cardinal Magalón,
told me that my only fault was that I was a Spaniard.

To this, I replied, "With all due respect, your Holiness,
that is my only virtue."

CHAPTER 26

From Rome she goes to Naples.

After a month and a half in Rome, I left for Naples on the fifth of July, 1626. We set sail from Ripa.

And one day in Naples, as I was strolling about the wharves, I was struck by the tittering laughter of two ladies, who leaned against a wall making conversation with two young bucks. They looked at me, and I looked at them, and one said, "Señora Catalina, where are you going, all by your lonesome?"

"My dear harlots," I replied, "I have come to deliver one hundred strokes to your pretty little necks, and a hundred gashes with this blade to the fool who would defend your honor."

The women fell dead silent, and then they hurried off.